Ethnic Policy in China
Is Reform Inevitable?

About the East-West Center

The East-West Center promotes better relations and understanding among the people and nations of the United States, Asia, and the Pacific through cooperative study, research, and dialogue. Established by the US Congress in 1960, the Center serves as a resource for information and analysis on critical issues of common concern, bringing people together to exchange views, build expertise, and develop policy options.

The Center's 21-acre Honolulu campus, adjacent to the University of Hawai'i at Mānoa, is located midway between Asia and the US mainland and features research, residential, and international conference facilities. The Center's Washington, DC, office focuses on preparing the United States for an era of growing Asia Pacific prominence.

The Center is an independent, public, nonprofit organization with funding from the US government, and additional support provided by private agencies, individuals, foundations, corporations, and governments in the region.

Policy Studies
an East-West Center series

Series Editors
Edward Aspinall and Dieter Ernst

Description
Policy Studies presents scholarly analysis of key contemporary domestic
and international political, economic, and strategic issues affecting Asia
in a policy relevant manner. Written for the policy community, academics, journalists, and the informed public, the peer-reviewed publications in this series provide new policy insights and perspectives based
on extensive fieldwork and rigorous scholarship.

The East-West Center is pleased to announce that
the Policy Studies series has been accepted for in-
dexing in Web of Science Book Citation Index.
The Web of Science is the largest and most com-
prehensive citation index available.

Notes to Contributors
Submissions may take the form of a proposal or complete manuscript.
For more information on the Policy Studies series, please contact the
Series Editors.

Editors, Policy Studies
East-West Center
1601 East-West Road
Honolulu, Hawai'i 96848-1601
Tel: 808.944.7197
Publications@EastWestCenter.org
EastWestCenter.org/PolicyStudies

Policy
Studies | 68

Ethnic Policy in China

Is Reform Inevitable?

James Leibold

Ethnic Policy in China: Is Reform Inevitable?
James Leibold

ISSN 1547-1349 (print) and 1547-1330 (electronic)
ISBN 978-0-86638-233-5 (print) and 978-0-86638-234-2 (electronic)

Hard copies of all titles, and free electronic copies of most titles, are available from:

Publication Sales Office
East-West Center
1601 East-West Road
Honolulu, Hawai'i 96848-1601
Tel: 808.944.7145
Fax: 808.944.7376
EWCBooks@EastWestCenter.org
EastWestCenter.org/PolicyStudies

In Asia, hard copies of all titles, and electronic copies of select Southeast Asia titles, co-published in Singapore, are available from:

Institute of Southeast Asian Studies
30 Heng Mui Keng Terrace
Pasir Panjang Road, Singapore 119614
publish@iseas.edu.sg
bookshop.iseas.edu.sg

Contents

List of Acronyms

3/14	March 14, 2008, Lhasa riots
7/5	July 5, 2009, Ürümqi riots
CASS	Chinese Academy of Social Sciences
CCTV	China Central Television
CLSG	Central Leading Small Group
CPC	Communist Party of China
CPPCC	Chinese People's Political Consultative Conference
EAI	East Asian Institute [National University of Singapore]
GDP	Gross Domestic Product
HDI	Human Development Index
NDU	National Defense University
PBSC	Politburo Standing Committee
PLA	People's Liberation Army
PRC	People's Republic of China
SEAC	State Ethnic Affairs Commission

TAR	Tibetan Autonomous Region
UFWD	United Front Work Department
XUAR	Xinjiang Uyghur Autonomous Region

Executive Summary

Balancing ethnocultural diversity and dignity with national integration and interethnic cohesion has been a constant challenge for Chinese policymakers. With a sizeable ethnic minority population, China has long been engaged in this delicate balancing act. Despite episodic conflict, it could be argued that the Communist Party of China (CPC) has, especially since the 1976 death of Mao Zedong, done a relatively competent job of containing ethnic tensions.

There are, however, signs that interethnic conflict may be growing as free-market forces and increased interethnic communication and mobility intensifies ethnic-based competition. For many Chinese the bloody riots in Lhasa (2008), Shaoguan (2009), and Ürümqi (2009) belie the party-state's claims of "harmonious ethnic relations."

Most Chinese thinkers condemn the lack of interethnic cohesion

In fact, interethnic conflict and violence is now seen as a sign of policy failure by a significant segment of the Chinese population.

Amid this perception of crisis, Chinese academics, policymakers, and other thought-leaders are engaged in unprecedented debate over the future direction of their country's ethnic policies. New online platforms and the commercialization of old media has engendered an explosion of information and discussion about this once-secretive and still highly sensitive topic.

As part of the larger search for indigenous and innovative solutions to contemporary problems, Chinese thinkers are exploring a range of new ideas for managing ethnic relations. Some of these ideas are rooted in Chinese tradition and others are based on what are viewed as global norms. Instead of strengthening minority rights and autonomy, as those in the West have long advocated, most Chinese thinkers condemn the lack of interethnic cohesion and believe urgent action is now required to preserve China's fragile national unity.

This study explores the last five years of domestic Chinese opinion on ethnic policies. Past debate is reviewed and implications for the future of ethnic policy under Xi Jinping and China's new fifth-generation of leadership are considered. National opinion is seen to be gradually coalescing on the need to rethink, if not fundamentally alter, existing policies to reinforce interethnic solidarity.

China's intellectuals increasingly agree that the current "divide and rule" tactics, inherited from the former Union of Soviet Socialist Republics (USSR), are out of touch with both Chinese tradition and global norms. A "melting pot" model is increasingly being accepted as better for de-emphasizing ethnic consciousness, improving ethnic relations, and solidifying national unity in the long run.

For over a decade Professor Ma Rong of Peking University has championed the cause of ethnic-policy reform. His once-marginal views are now part of the mainstream conversation with a wide range of academics, policymakers, and other thinkers (across ethnic and ideological spectrums) sharing his concerns with the current approach. Although prescriptions for reform vary, key liberals including Liu Junning, Li Datong, and Qin Hui agree with left-leaning voices like Wang Hui and Kong Qingdong about the need to chart a new course.

Hoping to avoid the sorts of ethnic implosions that occurred in the former USSR and in Yugoslavia, these individuals have offered proposals for strengthening national cohesion and belonging. Leading futurologist and policy expert Hu Angang recently surprised his colleagues when he called for a "second generation of ethnic policies" that would have wide-ranging implications for minority and majority communities alike.

Despite this vocal support for change, the party-state insists, at least publicly, that current policies are working and that any ethnic tensions are the result of outside interference. Interests deeply vested in the status quo resist significant change.

There are, however, now individuals in the top echelons of the CPC openly advocating new directions in ethnic policies, and they are looking to the new leadership for action. Xi Jinping's "Chinese dream" narrative stresses the unity and coalescence of public sentiment as a part of the great revival of the Chinese nation/race. Yet current ethnic policies remain the legacy of Hu Jintao and his mentor Hu Yaobang and are likely to be carefully guarded by their protégés and the ethnic-policy establishment.

Radical shifts in policy, such as ending regional ethnic autonomy or minority preferences, are unlikely in the near future. Even if the political will exists at the top of the CPC leadership, ethnic policy remains a relatively low priority. The complexities of the Chinese political system also make any bold new initiatives problematic. Regime stability—the party's abiding focus—requires social stability, and thus increased security efforts in troubled frontier regions are more likely than major policy changes.

> *Radical shifts in policy, such as ending regional ethnic autonomy or minority preferences, are unlikely in the near future*

That said, small but significant policy adjustments are seen as possible under Xi Jinping. These could include the removal of ethnic status from third-generation identification cards, increased study and use of China's official Putonghua language, and increased ethnic mobility as an element in changes to the household-registration system.

Reformers (both inside and outside the system) largely agree that change must proceed through gradual step-by-step consensus building. Any sweeping changes to current policy would require amendment to the constitution of the People's Republic of China. This would damage the party's reputation in the eyes of many ethnic minorities as well as the international community. Should, however, systematic ethnic unrest become widespread, the CPC could be forced into more fundamental changes.

Ethnic Policy in China
Is Reform Inevitable?

Introduction

Balancing ethnocultural diversity and dignity with national integration and social cohesion has been a constant challenge for Chinese policy-makers. Today's world of network connectivity is marked by a proliferation of "identity-based movements" where cultural, ethnic, and religious differences assume new saliency and complicate state- and nation-building projects (Castells 2010). As in other multiethnic countries, management of ethnic relations has long been a top policy imperative for the Chinese party-state, with China's unique history, geography, and demography shaping the cultural landscape for Chinese thought and policy on ethnic diversity.

> *Management of ethnic relations has long been a top policy imperative for the Chinese party-state*

According to eminent sociologist Fei Xiaotong, China exhibits a unique national form: what he described as the "multiple origins, one body" (多元一体) composition of the Chinese people. While consciousness of this national form is relatively recent, its "pluralistic yet unified configuration" is "the result of a historical process of millennia" (Fei 1988). Over three thousand years ago, a nucleus of Chinese civilization in the fertile Yellow River Valley began expanding as it drew in and fused with surrounding peoples, growing larger and larger like "a rolling snowball" (滚雪球) that was only restricted by natural ecological and geographic limits. The result is today's Chinese nation/race (中华民族)—a mosaic of fifty-six distinct, indivisible, and theoretically equal ethnic constituencies or *minzu* (民族) in Chinese parlance.[1]

Yet, in reality, the ethnic pieces of China's multicultural puzzle are neither fully commensurate nor necessarily harmonious. The People's Republic of China (PRC) hosts a single supermajority with 92 percent of its nearly 1.4 billion people officially classified as Han (汉族). The remaining 114 million people belong to one of fifty-five other diverse ethnic communities. These are collectively known as ethnic minorities (少数民族): each ranging from a few thousand to several million people who, while concentrated along China's strategic and resource-rich border regions, are spread across the nation.

Despite episodic conflict, it could be argued that the Communist Party of China (CPC) has, especially since the 1976 death of Mao Zedong, done a relatively competent job of containing ethnic tensions among these groups. However, there are signs this containment may be faltering as free-market forces intensify interethnic communication, competition, and mobility. In fact, according to Nicholas Bequelin (2012), the "most severe" interethnic violence in decades marred the ten-year rule (2002–12) of President Hu Jintao and Premier Wen Jiabao, with a string of disturbing incidents in Tibet, Xinjiang, Inner Mongolia, and interior provinces like Guangdong and Henan.

Since 2008 Chinese academics, policymakers, and thought-leaders have been engaged in an unprecedented (and increasingly vocal) debate over ethnic policy. Interethnic conflict and violence are viewed by many as signs of policy failure, and as part of the larger search for indigenous and innovative solutions to contemporary problems, Chinese thinkers are exploring a range of new ideas for managing ethnic relations. Some of these ideas are rooted in Chinese tradition while others are based on perceived global norms.

Instead of supporting the strengthening of minority rights and autonomy, as many in the West (Mackerras 2006; Barnett 2009; Sautman 2010 and 2012) have long advocated, Chinese thinkers tend to decry the lack of interethnic cohesion and argue that urgent action is required to shore up national unity. These voices, however, are seldom heard and poorly understood outside China, with state propaganda and dissident opinions shaping many of the perceptions the West has about ethnic issues in China.

Scope and Aims

By being attentive to the full range of Chinese commentary, this study seeks to gauge domestic Chinese opinion on ethnic policies. Internal Chinese debate concerning ethnic policies and relations is first reviewed and then its implications for the future direction of ethnic policy under Xi Jinping are explored. Analysis is based on a close reading of public commentary (both academic and popular) across a broad spectrum of Chinese society as well as on off-the-record discussions with China-based academics and their students.

To establish manageable limits, this work has excluded Chinese and Western analysts writing from areas outside the Chinese mainland and Hong Kong. Current Chinese thinking on ethnic issues, however, clearly has been influenced by experiences and voices from outside of China and this is noted where it is believed to be relevant. The study also puts to one side the implications of any changes in policy and the views of non-elite minorities, as these important topics have already been addressed in the development studies and human rights literature, although much more needs to be done here as well.

Chinese public opinion is notoriously difficult to accurately gauge (Tang 2005: 33–52), especially on such a sensitive issue as ethnic policy. Few Chinese are willing to speak frankly and openly with foreign researchers concerning such issues and most survey data and questionnaires avoid ethnic topics altogether.

Yet the scope of Sinophone discourse on ethnic matters has greatly expanded over the last decade. Once-restricted opinions and topics can now be found across China's dynamic new-media landscape. Commercial imperatives and new platforms have produced an "explosion of information" and social debate that the party-state is no longer able to fully control (Shirk 2011: 2). Much of this discussion occurs online in blogs, discussion forums, and commercial news portals but it is also increasingly seen in more mainstream books, newspapers, and progressive magazines.

As noted by William Callahan (2013), these conversations provide new opportunities for China watchers and others interested in Chinese politics. Rather than trying to "eavesdrop" on the politburo and its secret discussions through the outdated methods once used for studying the Soviet Kremlin, effort is now better spent listening to "what Chinese people are saying to each other in public spaces" (Ibid: 4–5). Callahan identifies a new group of "citizen intellectuals," who are strategically positioned between party-state officials and dissident agitators, and thus able to actively probe the limits of acceptable discourse while discussing "a multitude of different dreams, possibilities, and futures for China" (Ibid: 13).

Following Callahan, this study attempts to identify the attitudes of contemporary academics, policymakers, and other intellectuals on ethnic policy from publicly available sources and then evaluate the likely impact of these attitudes on state policy. The high-profile citizen intellectuals discussed in this study now have a disproportional influence on Chinese society and increasingly help shape public policy.

This study also attempts to recast China's ethnic policies and associated debates within the discursive and cultural milieu of Chinese thought and representations. Contemporary China exhibits a rich mélange of ideas. Liberalism and socialism now compete with more communitarian and indigenous paradigms of knowledge. Chinese thinkers have long struggled with how best to apply different ideas (particularly foreign ones) to their country's unique national condition (国情). Many today search for the China model (中国模式) or, more recently, the Chinese road (中国道路) or Chinese dream (中国梦).

As June Dreyer (1999) reminds us, this quest for an indigenous approach to ethnic issues is likely to occur within a "monocultural paradigm"—one that values unity over diversity and seeks to transform ethnocultural heterogeneity through the superiority of Chinese cultural norms. This traditional worldview, many of China's contemporary thinkers now believe, is broadly out of sync with current Soviet-derived ethnic polices as well as with Western theories and practices of multiculturalism. When viewed in this light, Chinese domestic opinion is gradually coalescing on the need to rethink, if not fundamentally reform, current ethnic policies to reinforce interethnic cohesion. New strategies, Chinese thought-leaders would have us believe, are now required to restore and continue China's three-thousand-year history of ethnic fusion (民族融合). In short, the "snowball" of interethnic solidary that Fei

> *The quest for an indigenous approach to ethnic issues is likely to occur within a 'monocultural paradigm'*

Xiaotong once spoke of requires renewed compacting, and Chinese thinkers are now putting forward a range of new ideas on how this might occur.

Current Policy and Perceived Shortcomings

China's current ethnic policies are rooted in Marxist-Leninist theory and the past experience of the Union of Soviet Socialist Republics (USSR). The so-called national question (民族问题) or, more precisely, the problem of dealing with minority communities, is viewed in accordance with the "scientific laws of historical materialism" (Connor 1984). Modernity is a linear path but not all peoples are capable of progressing at the same rate. This means ethnocultural distinctions will only disappear following the final victory of the revolution.

To guard against majority chauvinism and secure the loyalty of often strategically placed ethnic minorities, the Bolsheviks afforded them protections and state recognition within the framework of a multi-ethnic and federated political structure. In the USSR, the Bolsheviks created forms of nationhood (national cultures, elites, languages, and territories) for non-Russian minorities—ultimately creating what Terry Martin (2001) termed the world's first "Affirmative Action Empire."

In contrast to claims that China slavishly imitated (亦步亦趋) Soviet policies, the CPC did "sinicize" some important aspects of Marxist-Leninist theory on the national question. Mao Zedong and other Chinese communist leaders ultimately rejected any form of territorial succession or federalism for China's minorities. Instead, given the overwhelming percentage of the majority Han population, they opted for a more circumscribed form of ethnic autonomy (Leibold 2007: 81–109). The PRC Constitution provides, on paper at least, a range of distinct legal protections for minority communities. These include, in the current 1982 version, "the freedom to use and develop their own spoken and written languages, and to preserve or reform their own ways and customs" and the right to practice "regional autonomy" in "areas where people of minority nationalities live in compact communities."

This is a marked departure from the way ethnocultural variation was earlier viewed in imperial China. In Confucian orthodoxy, difference is a transitory and elastic state which may be transformed through normative learning and changes in lifestyle. The boundary between Chineseness (夏) and barbarism (夷) is mercurial and determined by culture (Confucian civility versus barbarian incivility) and ecology (sedentary lifestyle versus pastoral nomadism) rather than by any modern sense of ethnicity or nationality.

At times of disunity or state weakness this boundary could harden, with the barbarians identified as possessing a different nature (性) or life force (气), but the normative ideal remained one of transformation, fusion, and ultimately unity: an inclusive, all-under-heaven (*tianxia* 天下) state of hierarchical harmony. The Chinese Academy of Social Sciences (CASS) philosopher Zhao Tingyang (2005) argues this state of *tianxia* defined Chinese tradition and could serve as a future model of global governance (Callahan 2013: 52–58). Here strategies of indirect rule, such as the loose rein (羈縻) or native chieftain (土司) systems of the imperial past and contemporary practices of affirmative action and ethnic autonomy, are viewed as expedient and temporary, with the superior aura of Chinese civilization expected to eventually draw in and gradually erase ethnocultural difference (Leibold 2007: 19–24).

Three Key Policy Planks

In contrast, today's Chinese policy is premised, in theory at least, on preserving ethnic diversity and gradual, state-guided, development—allowing each group to progress toward socialist modernity on its own terms and at its own pace.

This system of stewardship includes three interlinking policy elements: 1) the identification and classification of ethnic groups (民族识别); 2) a system of regional ethnic autonomy (民族区域自治制度); and 3) a series of preferential minority-treatment policies (民族优惠政策). Even if never fully implemented, this policy architecture guides the way ethnic diversity is formally discussed and currently handled within China and, despite some weakening during the Great Leap Forward (1958–62) and the Cultural Revolution (1966–76), this architecture was strengthened and institutionalized following the 1976 death of Mao.

Policy implementation required the party-state to first determine the number of ethnic groups in China so that they could be fully protected and represented in national life. During the early 1950s Beijing dispatched teams of ethnologists across the nation to identify, classify, and chronicle the new nation-state's ethnic diversity. The result was a growing number of officially recognized ethnic groups until, during the early 1980s, the count stabilized at fifty-six (Mullaney 2011).

While not all of these categories originally represented unified, self-ascribed communities, their institutionalization over the course of CPC rule solidified the importance of these labels in the daily lives and minds of Chinese citizens. Residents of China today have their ethnic category clearly marked on their personal identification cards and must include this information on all official documents (Gladney 2004).

Minority groups living together in concentrated numbers are entitled to the right of regional autonomy. This right was first enshrined in the 1954 PRC Constitution and, in 1984, became part of the national legal code with the passage of the "Law on Regional Ethnic Autonomy." Depending on the size and density of a minority community, the state has created autonomous units at various administrative levels. These self-governing units are permitted (in theory, again) to interpret, adapt, and implement state policies "in light of specific local conditions," which could include the extension of special provisions aimed at preserving diversity and promoting equality. By 2005 more than 71 percent of China's minority population lived within one of the more-than-1,300 autonomous units that covered 64 percent of Chinese territory (Huang and Zhang 2007).

Since 1949 the CPC has also extended special rights and privileges to the non-Han population regardless of where they live. Today these policies include preferential access to employment, higher education, and political

> *Since 1949 the CPC has extended special rights and privileges to the non-Han population*

office; certain exceptions from family planning restrictions; special tax breaks; and the right to protect and use their own culture, language, and religion (Mackerras 2003; Sautman 2010).

In the area of education, for example, many minority students receive extra points added to their scores on the national university entrance exam (高考) and tuition waivers and living-expense stipends once enrolled at university. Judicially, minority criminals receive more lenient treatment under the "two restrains [in arrests and executions] and one leniency [in treatment]" (两少一宽) policy. This is, however, balanced by unyielding punishment of any behavior identified as anti-state or subversive.

Finally the state provides massive subsidies (through both the national treasury and regional-pairing schemes) to boost economic development in minority regions. In 2009 this ranged from 29–94 percent of the total annual budgets of the five provincial-level autonomous regions (Ma 2010: 10–11). Tibet, for example, has received nearly US$14 billion in central expenditures since the establishment of the Tibetan Autonomous Region (TAR) in 1965 (Wang L. 2008a: 28).

Policy Shortcomings

Despite this regime of state promotion and protection, minority populations (in aggregate) remain significantly behind their Han counterparts on nearly all objective standards of development—education, health and welfare indicators, and income. This is particularly evident among rural Uyghur and Tibetan communities.

Fiscal transfers have dramatically boosted Gross Domestic Product (GDP) growth rates in frontier regions but disproportionate numbers of minorities continue to live in isolated, poverty-stricken, rural communities. Over 50 percent of officially designated improvised counties (贫困县) are in rural areas with high proportions of non-Han minorities (Zhu and Blachford 2012: 725; Freeman 2013: 18). Despite nearly doubling since 1949, life expectancy in the TAR remains eight years below the national average (Xinhua 2011b), and twelve years behind for Uyghurs in Xinjiang (Mackerras 2012: 500). Current research by Bhalla and Luo (2013) identifies significant gaps in access to health and education resources among minorities versus Han communities.

But overgeneralizations are dangerous. Many minorities, especially those in the nation's southwest, have benefited significantly from current state policies, and feel a sense of kinship with the Han majority. Still, the current approach has been less successful in cultivating a sense of national belonging among key segments of the Uyghur and Tibetan communities and, to a lesser extent, among some Hui and Mongol minorities.

Through an aggressive cultivation of minority cadres, the CPC now claims over 5 million minority members—6.6 percent of total CPC membership (Leibold 2012). Some, such as Vice Foreign Minister Fu Ying or new Secretary-General of the State Council Yang Jing (both Mongols), have risen to important positions of authority. However, many others hold largely ceremonial positions devoid of any real decision-making authority.

There are, for example, only ten minority members of the current Central Committee (4.9%), the smallest number since 1973. There have only been four minority members of the politburo since 1949, and not a single non-Han member of the Politburo Standing Committee (PBSC). PRC law requires that the heads of each autonomous unit come from the minority group for which it is named, yet these state positions are ultimately subordinate to predominantly Han party secretaries (Cheng L. 2008).

The place of non-Han minorities within Chinese society is hindered by the relative demographics of the majority and minority communities: the ethnic minorities are like scattered drops of oil within a massive sea of Hanness. The Han (when one includes military and security personal and their dependents) now make up a majority in every province and provincial-level autonomous region except Tibet.

> *The ethnic minorities are like scattered drops of oil within a massive sea of Hanness*

Since 1949 Han transmigration (both state-sponsored and self-initiated) has fundamentally altered the ethnic spatiality of China. This has left fewer autonomous spaces for non-Han culture and rendered minority representation largely formulaic and hollow. The sheer scale of Han society ensures that the CPC's minority protections remain under constant threat.

In the more open, free-wheeling, and market-driven environment of post-Mao China, the party-state finds it increasingly difficult to maintain a firm grip on ethnic safeguards and promote interethnic harmony. To date, its most effective tool has been stability maintenance (维稳): locking down and securitizing trouble-spots, controlling (and at times cutting off) communications, and placing institutional barriers on interethnic contact and mobility.

Against this backdrop, the only way forward, critics of current ethnic policies argue, is state-guided integration rather than continued isolation and further marginalization. These critics advocate a return to and re-forging of the *Datong* (大同, Grand Union) where ethnocultural diversity fuses (融合) into a singular, cohesive, body politic.

For many Chinese intellectuals, the shocking violence that erupted in Ürümqi in July 2009 served as a forceful reminder of the perilous state of this Grand Union and of the urgent need for reform.

"China's 9/11": The Ürümqi Riots

On the evening of July 5, 2009, the streets of Ürümqi erupted in bloodshed as the capital of the far-west XUAR witnessed one of the deadliest incidents of communal violence in decades (Millward 2009).[2] For many Chinese citizens the events of 7/5 were "China's 9/11": a premeditated terrorist attack planned and orchestrated from abroad by hostile anti-China forces. The attack resulted in "the blood-thirsty maiming and slaughter of civilians, as young as six years old, in Ürümqi" (Li H. 2009).

Yet existing evidence paints a different picture: that of a spontaneous and turbulent ethnic riot, one that pitted Uyghurs against Han in running street battles while security forces struggled unsuccessfully to maintain control.

The unrest began with a peaceful demonstration by over a thousand Uyghurs in People's Square in Ürümqi. They called for an investigation into an earlier, equally brutal, riot at the Xuri Toy Factory thousands of miles away in Shaoguan, Guangdong. There two Uyghur employees had been killed and hundreds injured (many seriously) after Han workers rampaged following a cascade of rumors concerning the alleged rape of a female Han employee. Fueled by social media, more rumors, and photographic/video "evidence" that reportedly showed a far greater death toll, Uyghur co-ethnics protested in Ürümqi. While accurate details remain sketchy, this initially peaceful protest quickly turned ugly.

As darkness approached, the city descended into a macabre theatre of violence: marauding Uyghur youth hunted down and then butchered innocent Han civilians (or those perceived to be Han) with knives, pipes, and other improvised weapons. Hundreds of vehicles and shops were looted and then set ablaze while government security forces floundered in their attempts to control the situation. Sporadic violence continued throughout the night and the following days. Security personal rounded up thousands of Uyghur residents. Meanwhile, Han vigilantes took to the streets seeking to mete out revenge on Uyghur miscreants while guarding their own neighborhoods.

Seeking to regain control, regional authorities locked down the city and cut Internet and phone service as thousands of armed security forces took up positions across the city and in other regional centers to prevent further conflict. President Hu Jintao left the G8 Summit in Italy to convene an emergency meeting of the politburo while PBSC security czar Zhou Yongkang was dispatched to Xinjiang. Government sources claim that 197 people (134 described as "innocent" Han civilians) were killed in the rioting with a further 1,721 injured. Others claim that the actual death toll was much higher, with upwards of a thousand killed (Carlson 2009).

To many in China, the 7/5 Incident proved the failure of current ethnic policies. This is especially so when it is viewed alongside other incidents of ethnic unrest such as the March 14, 2008, riots in Lhasa (the "3/14 Incident") and other Tibetan regions; protests in Xilinhot, Inner Mongolia, in May 2011; and the over-one-hundred Tibetan self-immolations since March 2012.

> *To many in China, the 7/5 Incident proved the failure of current ethnic policies*

Unlike previous incidents pitting minority protesters against the state security forces, the Lhasa, Shaoguan, and Ürümqi incidents involved vicious attacks on Han civilians and their businesses. As Sautman (2010: 52; 2012) demonstrates, these incidents "had a huge effect in generating a national discourse in China about ethnic policies." The scale and brutality of the violence shocked most Chinese while reinforcing majority stereotypes and fears of knife-wielding Tibetan and Uyghur "savages." There is little on which the maverick artist Ai Weiwei (2008) and the ultra-nationalist personality Kong Qingdong (2011b) agree—but they both blame the CPC's ethnic policies for communal tensions, claiming the state is no longer capable of maintaining harmonious ethnic relations.

Making Sense of Recent Unrest

Publicly at least, the CPC believes its ethnic policies are working fine. "In the entire world," former TAR Chairman Qiangba Puncog stated, "it's difficult to find ethnic policies as exemplary as ours" (Chen 2012). In summarizing the Hu-Wen era, the Leading Party Group of the State Ethnic Affairs Commission (SEAC) concludes: "The decade since the holding of the Sixteenth National Congress of the CPC has witnessed great progress in China's ethnic initiatives… [the CPC] has united and led people of all ethnic groups in a pioneering surge forward, bringing about new economic and social advances among ethnic minority groups and in ethnic minority areas" (Leading Group of the SEAC 2012). The imagery here is that of a colorful yet harmonic mosaic, like the fifty-six children who carried the PRC flag across the Bird's Nest Stadium during the opening ceremony of the Beijing Olympics.

According to CPC officials, any ethnic tensions are the result of "outside interference"—separatists and their foreign supporters who seek to incite division and derail China's peaceful rise. The party-state's 2009 *White Paper* on ethnic policy, released following the 7/5 Incident, confidently declared: "Sixty years of experiences have proved that China's ethnic policies are correct and effective and are in keeping with China's actual conditions and the common interests of all ethnic groups, winning the support of the people of all ethnic groups" (State Council 2009). "The violent crimes in Ürümqi have nothing to do with China's ethnic policies," a SEAC official told reporters, and thus do not necessitate any change in direction (AFP 2009).

Outside top party circles, however, few agree. "Ostrich talk," is what leading public intellectual Zhu Xueqin concluded regarding the government's response to the 7/5 Incident. With its head stuck in the sand, the Chinese state is incapable of appreciating how its ethnic policies are out-of-date and incapable of stemming the tide of ethnic conflict (RFI 2009). This troubling spike in violence, Hong Kong's influential *Oriental Daily* newspaper declared (*Oriental Daily* 2009), indicates a "powder-keg" of ethnic contradictions that poses a serious threat to social stability, and that the government's policy of "blind appeasement" is increasingly outmoded.

During an interview following the 3/14 Incident, Ai Weiwei (2008) asserted that the rioting "proves in any case that [China's] ethnic minority policies have failed… in the past we Han demolished their temples and now they smash our houses and attack us." Similarly, Kong Qingdong (2011b) identified ethnic relations as one of five potential stumbling blocks for China and, in place of current policy, suggested "that Xinjiang develop activities like Chongqing and sing red songs and attack corruption so that all the ethnic groups in Xinjiang can unite together under the party's Central Committee and become single-minded with all the country's people."

Not since the early 1980s have individuals across ethnic and ideological divides so openly discussed the health of ethnic relations in China. This sensitive and often-secretive topic has elicited intense debate since 2008, with much of the discussion revolving around the controversial opinions offered by Peking University Professor Ma Rong.

The Reform Agenda and Discontents

For over a decade Ma Rong has questioned the efficacy of the party-state's current ethnic policies. He has called for gradual yet urgent adjustments (调整) to forestall a possible national tragedy: the territorial/ethnic dismemberment of China. An "academic princeling" of sorts, Ma Rong is the son of Ma Yin, a veteran Hui ethnic revolutionary who, before his death in 1991, became a leading scholar and policymaker inside the SEAC.

Ma Rong's academic career was nurtured and supported by Chinese sociologist Fei Xiaotong following Fei's rehabilitation and appointment in 1985 as the director of the resurrected Institute of Sociology at Peking University. Ma completed his PhD dissertation on ethnic migration and integration in rural Chifeng, Inner Mongolia, under the supervision of Sidney Goldstein at Brown University in the United States in 1987, and then went on to become a professor and then director and dean of sociology at Peking University.

A cautious and sophisticated thinker, Ma Rong advocates a distinctly sociological approach to ethnicity in China. Heavily influenced by modernization theory and the sociology pioneered by Emile Durkheim, Ma Rong frequently cites Nathan Glazer, Milton Gordon, Daniel Moynihan, and other American sociologists of ethnicity who raised concerns about the rising tide of ethnic consciousness in the wake of the civil rights movement in the United States. Like these scholars, Ma Rong might be labeled a "neo-conservative" in today's parlance, yet his views on identity more closely align with classic liberal thought. Since John Stuart Mill, such thought has stressed the importance of individual over group rights and viewed ethnocultural identity as a personal matter and thus inappropriate for state politicization (Barry 2001: 112–54; Sautman 2012: 18).

Ma Rong speaks of the "modern, legal, civic state" as "an inevitable trend of human development" (Ma 2012: 68) with this sort of linear, teleological, temporality deeply rooted in modern Chinese thought (Duara 1995) and foundational to the CPC's "civilizing project" among its frontier minorities (Harrell 1995). For Ma Rong, however, what others call Hanification (汉化) is simply the inexorable process of modernization: the adoption of modern, universal norms which has occurred in China since the Opium War (1839-42), albeit at different rates among Chinese ethnic groups (Ma 2012: 254–63).

> *For Ma Rong, however, what others call Hanification is simply the inexorable process of modernization*

The new high-rises transforming the landscape of Kashgar and Lhasa are not "Han-style constructions" but simply modern buildings with reinforced concrete and glass windows similar to other office towers around the globe. Equivalent commentary could be offered concerning the now-ubiquitous Western business suit. As "forerunners" of progress and modern culture, the Han have simply been the early adopters of these "Western" styles, in Ma Rong's view, and as China continues to develop and open up to the world, these universal norms will spread throughout minority communities and frontier regions. Yet, modernity does not mean uniformity, with Ma Rong insisting on the preservation of China's diverse cultural heritages.

The pace of social transformation in China today has simply outstripped government policy, Ma argues. He insists that government policy is increasingly out of touch with global norms and Chinese tradition, and must alter accordingly. Through prolific scholarship, years of persistent advocacy, and a legion of students and supporters, Ma Rong's once-eccentric views now permeate much of contemporary Sinophone discourse on ethnic relations and policy.

Ma Rong's Case for Reform

What is *minzu* (民族)? Ma Rong's analysis begins with this conceptual problem. The Chinese term *minzu* is numerically imprecise and currently used to refer to both the collective unity of the Chinese nation/race (中华民族) and to its fifty-six ethnic communities (五十六个民族). This leads not only to semantic confusion, Ma Rong argues (2012: 3–6), but also traps ethnic identity within stagnant and reified state categories.

In English there is a clear conceptual difference between a "nation," which is a civic-territorial unit within the current nation-state system, and "ethnic groups," who possess a shared culture (customs, language, religion, and/or territory) but live within one or more nations. If ethnic groups in China exist at the same level as the Chinese nation they should be entitled to "self-determination" or even independence, as some in the West have long argued.

To resolve this problem Ma Rong puts forward the neologism *zuqun* (族群) to refer to the different ethnic communities within China while reserving the term *minzu* (民族) for discussing the Chinese nation as a whole. Strictly speaking, China is a multiethnic society (多族群社会) rather than a state of multiple nations. This confused lexicon, Ma asserts, reflects the general weakness of China's post-1949 nation-building process.

Like the United States during its Civil War, contemporary China is a house divided. Ma Rong argues (2012: 168–91) that the fragile state of ethnic relations in China is now the nation's "biggest social issue." Through a range of well-intentioned but ultimately misguided policies, the party-state has unwittingly created two Chinas: Han China and minorities China. The education system, for example, is divided into "ordinary schools" for Han students and "*minzu* schools" where minority students can be educated in their native languages from primary school through university. This helps preserve languages and cultures but isolates minority students from mainstream society.

The result, according to Ma Rong, is students with poor proficiency in the national language (普通话, Putonghua) who are unable to compete in the market economy and labor market. In the realm of culture, minorities have their own celebrations and festivals, films, sporting competitions, and television shows—but there is little ethnocultural diversity within mainstream entertainment. Han producers and artists avoid ethnic topics for fear of offending minority sensitivities. This Han/minority "dual structure" (二元结构), Ma Rong asserts, amplifies ethnocultural differences and contributes to social conflict and a general lack of mutual interaction and understanding.

This lack of social cohesion is reflected in demographic data. Ma and his colleagues have highlighted the relatively low rate of Han/minority intermarriage, especially between the Han and religious minorities like the Uyghurs (Ma 1999; Li X. 2004). This is a reflection of the fact that Han and minority communities, especially in the northwest, continue to live and work largely in segregated communities with only limited daily interactions.

> *This Han/minority 'dual structure,' Ma Rong asserts, amplifies ethnocultural differences and contributes to social conflict*

Ma Rong is careful to employ the term "ethnic divisions" (民族区隔) rather than "segregation," although he does point to the negative effects of the system of racial segregation (种族隔离度) in the United States prior to the civil rights movement. Others writing in response to Ma Rong have suggested that China's *minzu* institutions function as "a uniquely Chinese system of ethnic apartheid," with the fifty-six *minzu* groups like "bamboo poles" or "small states" (Wenrui 2008). For Ma Rong, *minzu* groups act as tribal collectives (族集合体) within a deeply divided Chinese society (Ma 2012: 68).

These divisions, Ma Rong (2012: 1–34; 192–253) and others argue, are the product of ethnic policies adopted from the former USSR. By blindly following Soviet policymakers the CPC departed from "China's traditional route" where identity was marked against a dynamic "civilized-barbarian distinction continuum" with groups moving along the continuum through the adoption of more "advanced" Chinese culture.

In sharp contrast to this "culture-centered identity" or "universalism," Soviet-style policies politicize ethnicity by identifying and classifying *minzu* groups and then strengthening these differences through the system of regional autonomy and ethnic preferences. "The institutionalization of ethnic groups systematically creates institutional barriers for the interaction and integration between the members of different ethnic groups," Ma Rong writes (2007: 211) and "…always reminds them that they belong to 'a specific group'."

For Ma Rong this approach differs from the way identity operates in the United States, where the US Constitution endows citizen rights rather than group rights, preventing the politicization of ethnicity and encouraging more frequent interaction, intermarriage, and co-residency across ethnic lines. China should learn from this experience and "de-politicize" (去政治化) ethnic issues in order to consolidate its own national identity (Ma 2009b; 2012: 16–19).

Without a policy reversal, Ma Rong (2012: 192–253) contends, China could follow the USSR and Yugoslavia down the path of national disintegration. The other two countries collapsed from "faulty theory and system design." China must remain "vigilant in peaceful times" while recognizing that the Ürümqi and Lhasa riots were "a clear warning sign" that, with "a similar system design," China could share a similar fate.

Soviet leaders, from Stalin to Gorbachav, insisted their policies were correct and the "Soviet people" were a cohesive whole. Yet, when the opportunity presented itself, the entire edifice came crashing down, leaving Kremlin-watchers dumbfounded. According to Ma Rong, China possesses the same three prerequisites for disintegration (ethnic consciousness, ethnic leadership, and ethnic territory) and, with "anti-China forces" continually inciting ethnic divisions, China has no choice but to act. "At present," Ma Rong (2012: 224) asserts in a rather alarmist fashion, "the biggest danger China faces in the twenty-first century is the breakup of the country."

The blunt contrast Ma Rong draws between the Soviet and American "models" is open to interpretation and, at times, may be exaggerated by Ma. First, he overstates the role of ethnic issues in the collapse of the USSR (Sautman 2010: 91–95). Moreover, as viewed by many Western experts (Naughton and Yang 2004; Mackerras 2006; Shambaugh 2008: 161–81; Sautman 2010: 91), the lack of a federalist political structure and Han demographic dominance makes Chinese ethnic or territorial fragmentation unlikely. Lastly, internal Chinese security policies have greatly reduced the capacity of minority groups like the Uyghurs to "act collectively" (Bovington 2010).

Also Ma Rong holds an apparently overly idealistic view of US society. Such statements as: "In the last thirty years America has not made a film where you can only see purely white actors" (Ma 2012: 185) or "We must admit that America has definitely achieved success in harmonizing race relations since the 'civil rights movement'" (Ma 2009b) clearly overlook ongoing ethnic prejudice and even violence in the United States.

What specific policy adjustment does Ma Rong advocate? His language is guarded when writing in Chinese, especially for mainland publications. But in several (largely obscure) English language publications he suggests a new policy direction that would over time weaken (淡化) *minzu*-based consciousness and replace it with a collective sense of national belonging:

> …the policies in favor of minorities should continue, but the target of these policies should be gradually switched from 'all members of minority groups' to all residents of 'poor areas,' then to 'all individual citizens who need the help.' Similarly, the administrative structure of autonomous areas should be maintained for a period of time but the sense of a 'nationality's territory' should be reduced gradually. The dual system of schools in autonomous areas should continue, while various kinds of bilingual education facilities should be offered to all members of minority groups. The situation of ethnic stratification in Chinese society should be systematically studied and the government should establish programmes to help minority members who are disadvantaged in terms of language and other skills (Ma 2009a: np).

Ma is particularly critical of the CPC's policies of preferential treatment and stresses the need to move from ethnic favoritism (群体优惠) to individual support (个体扶助). According to Ma, such policies were only intended to be temporary measures and increasingly clash with free-market and liberal principles. They foster a culture of dependency and a lack of competitiveness within many minority communities and have unleashed a dangerous backlash of majority nationalism and resentment—especially among the large Han communities in Xinjiang.

In their place, Ma Rong (2011: 119, 123) advocates a set of "regional-support policies" and efforts to "facilitate and promote the cross flow of labors [*sic*] and all ethnic groups" with the ultimate aim of creating "a nationwide labor market." The growing economic and social gap between Han and minority communities means that the Chinese state must continue to play a leading role in subsidizing marginalized communities—but these programs should be *minzu*-blind and instead target localities and individuals in need.

Ma Rong is conscious of the need to move slowly and build consensus among majority and minority communities alike. Yet, for him, reform is both necessary and inevitable.

A Second Generation of Ethnic Policies?

Ma Rong is no longer a lone voice for ethnic-policy reform—his views are increasingly echoed in academic and online writing, and are now shared by some top party officials. To date the most explicit call for change—and certainly the most controversial yet potentially influential—comes from futurologist and leading policy adviser Hu Angang. In late 2011 he appealed for a second generation of ethnic policies (第二代民族政策): ones that would attenuate ethnic identity (民族认同) and strengthen a single shared national/racial identity (国族认同) (Hu and Hu 2011).

Clearly influenced by Ma Rong's ideas, Hu Angang put forward the first systematic agenda for ethnic-policy reform, and in the process, stirred a hornet's nest of contention among academic and policy experts.

Hu Angang is the founding director of the Institute for Contemporary China Studies at Tsinghua University, one of China's most influential think tanks. Cheng Li (2011: xv–xl) of the Brookings Institution describes him as one of the most visionary and high-profile thinkers addressing China's rise and its associated problems. Ideologically, Hu is often depicted as left-of-center due to his support for state intervention in the economy and management of social issues, but his views (like most Chinese intellectuals) are eclectic yet decisively nationalistic.

Over the past decade, the party-state has adopted no fewer than seven major policy reforms initiated by Hu. Will ethnic policy be next? In an article originally published in Xinjiang Normal University's academic journal but since republished and discussed in key party magazines including *Seeking Truth* (*Qiushi,* 求实) and *Study Times* (*Xuexi Shibao,* 学习时报), as well as numerous other places across the Sinophone Internet, Hu Angang and his colleague at Tsinghua University, Hu Lianhe, speak of a major new policy orientation (方针).

> *The party-state has adopted no fewer than seven major policy reforms initiated by Hu. Will ethnic policy be next?*

The Tibet and Xinjiang Work Forums convened by the party's Central Committee in early 2010, they argue, signaled a new focus on "ethnic contact, exchange, and blending" (民族交往交流交融), which was one of the numerous phrases used by Hu Jintao in his addresses to both gatherings. While we know little about what was actually discussed at these two close-door meetings, which were attended by the entire politburo, current policies were surely debated vigorously in the wake of recent ethnic violence. Publicly, at least, the two meetings called for much of the same—with additional state funds and preferences aimed at promoting "leap frog" development in the two frontier regions in order to address livelihood issues thought to be contributing to current unrest (CECC 2010a; 2010b).

Surprisingly, however, Premier Wen Jiabao's yearly work report to the National People's Congress marked an important departure from previous years. For the first (and only) time, Wen's report, which was delivered in-between the Tibet and Xinjiang work forums in March 2010, failed to include the ritual mention of the system of regional ethnic autonomy, and instead stressed the importance of "strengthening national consciousness and civic education" in order to "oppose ethnic splittism and safeguard national unity" (Xinhua 2010). While the term returned in subsequent reports,[3] its omission in 2010 seemed to flag a new tone or direction in policy–something the two Hus and others quickly seized upon.

In their article, the two Hus warn of the twin dangers of regional ethnic elites (地方民族精英) and regional ethnic interest (地方民族利益). They contend that the failure to limit narrow ethnic consciousness in frontier regions such as Tibet and Xinjiang has increased the threat of ethnic separatism. Meanwhile, expressing double standards, Western nations criticize China for violating minority human rights while pursuing their own national policies of ethnic fusion.

In their eyes the choice confronting China is stark: continue to abide by the former USSR's "hors d'oeuvres"-style (大拼盘模式) ethnic policies and share

> *In their eyes the choice confronting China is stark: continue to abide by the former USSR's 'hors d'oeuvres'-style policies or move toward the global norm*

its fate or move toward the global norm by shifting to the melting pot formula (大熔炉模式) which has proven successful in Brazil, India, the United States, and other large countries.

Inside the melting pot, cultural pluralism (文化多元性) is tolerated and individuals are permitted to maintain their cultural traditions. Yet the absence of group-differentiated institutions, laws, or privileges encourages natural ethnic mingling and a shared sense of civic belonging. To forge China's own melting pot—a "you are in me, I am in you" cohesive force—the two Hus outline a number of bold policy initiatives.

First, politically: eliminating group-differentiated rights and obligations to ensure the equality of all citizens. This should include nationwide reform to territorial administrative divisions to increase market efficiencies; the removal of bureaucratic barriers; and a more balanced system of territorial governance in terms of ethnic mix, population, and size. Preferential state-aid should be based on relative impoverishment rather than ethnic status and ethnic markers should be removed from identification cards, job and school applications, and other official documents.

Second, economically: instigating new measures to increase economic interaction and ties between ethnic minority regions and the rest of the country. These frontier regions have been the greatest beneficiaries of China's economic reforms in terms of GDP and Human Development Index (HDI)-measured social welfare—but more is now required to remove institutional barriers to the free flow of capital, goods, information, and labor; increase competition, creative forces, and entrepreneurial initiatives; and reduce inefficiencies and regional gaps.

Third, culturally: increasing focus on integrating different ethnic traditions into a collective civic culture and identity. This will require the increased spoken and written use of the national language, guarding against religious extremism, greater attention to civic ceremonies fostering national identification, and other propaganda and media efforts consistent with these goals.

Fourth, socially: enhancing the flow of peoples across administrative boundaries in keeping with the current wave of globalization, modernization, and the increasing free flow of information. The mechanical nature of China's ethnic-classification system provides little opportunity for talented foreigners who wish to naturalize and become

Chinese citizens. Facilitating foreign immigration will not only benefit China's modernization but also serve to reduce the presumed identification of Han culture with Chinese culture, rendering China a more dynamic, inclusive, and robust society. Finally, new methods increasing ethnic mobility, co-residence, and intermarriage and promoting Putonghua, bilingual, and mixed-ethnic schooling are required.

The "Minzu Establishment" Responds

One of the best indictors of the growing influence of reformist opinion is the vigorous public reaction by what may be termed the "*minzu* establishment," those institutions and individuals with close ties to China's vast ethnic bureaucracy. Here one finds a large coterie of "scholar-cadres," who generally support the status quo even if they might, in private, disagree with certain aspects of current policy (Goldman and Cheek 1987: 3). In the first half of 2012, ethnic institutions across China convened forums to criticize the call for a second generation of ethnic policies.

In February 2012 the Institute of Ethnology and Anthropology at CASS held one such meeting where more than 40 experts from a range of *minzu* institutions, including representatives from the Central Committee's United Front Work Department (UFWD) and the SEAC, were reported to have gathered (Liu L. 2012).[4] Here the authority of Hu Angang and other reformers were questioned. Participants claimed that those advocating a second generation of ethnic policies "have never conducted in-depth studies on China's ethnic policy and on the actual development of China's ethnic regions."

Challenging the CPC's "basic policy and system" (as opposed to "specific policies"), some warned, was "both naïve and dangerous from a political perspective." Discussing ethnic issues "outside the basic policy framework" could lead to "ideological chaos" and even precipitate "a major political upheaval" or "unexpected events and disharmonious incidents." Scholars at the meeting argued that integration does not lead to homogeneity and stressed that artificial and impetuous "forced assimilation" (强制同化) would undermine the cooperation, solidarity, and trust central to solving ethnic issues in a multiethnic country such as China. Those that seek to alter current policies were described as either extreme leftists or pseudo-fascists seeking to pursue a Nazi-style policy of "one race, one state" (一个民族一个国家).

Gatherings like this one, and another symposium held at the Minzu University of China in April 2012, endorsed current policies as correct and labeled the reform agenda as "rash and imprudent" (Wu 2012). These forums concluded that, while occasional "perfecting" (完善) was required, past experience has proven that the current approach is best suited for China's unique "national conditions."

No one was criticized by name at these meetings. Rather code words, such as "second generation of ethnic policies" (*viz.* Hu An-gang and Hu Lianhe) and "de-politicization" (*viz.* Ma Rong), were employed to denounce those questioning the status quo. The two Hus have yet to respond publicly, but Ma Rong (2013) published a long article in January distancing himself from the two Hus while clarifying his own position.

Ma begins by welcoming their contribution to the debate—stressing the value of ideas from outside the narrow field of *minzu* studies; yet he agrees that it's premature to speak of a second generation of ethnic policies. Rather a more gradualist and cautious approach is required, one that builds consensus among minority elites for change and respects cultural diversity and the differing rates of development across China's vast territory. In a large, complex country like China, efforts to "cut everything with a single knife" (一刀切) or achieve a "great leap forward" (大跃进) are doomed to fail. At the same time, however, he mocks the sort of Maoist-style dogmatism, what used to be called the "two whatevers" (两个凡是, essentially whatever Mao said was correct), that now prevents individuals from questioning current ethnic policies and exploring new approaches.

Most of the serious theoretical effort in repudiating the reform agenda was taken up by the highly respected and influential Mongolian scholar Hao Shiyuan. As one of the deputy secretary generals of CASS (a ministerial-level state appointment) and the director of its Institute of Ethnology and Anthropology (as well as husband of Vice Foreign Minister Fu Ying), Hao speaks with the full weight of the *minzu* establishment behind him.

Over the course of two months in early 2012, Hao penned a series of four long (exceeding fifty thousand characters in total) critiques.[5] Citing sources from Lenin and Stalin to Deng Xiaoping and Hu Jin-tao, Hao stressed the importance of achieving substantive equality over mere formal or legal equality. Hao also highlighted the illegality of the reform agenda, pointing out that it violated the constitutional provision for genuine equality (真正的平等).

Much of Hao's critique attacked selective readings of international experiences and their lessons for China as offered by Ma Rong and the two Hus. In light of recent discussions of the "China model" or "Chinese road" it seems ironic that the core of the current mainstream ethnic-policy debate revolves around the suitability of foreign models while research on pre-modern Chinese views of ethnocultural diversity has been limited to more specialized academic publications.

Hao Shiyuan, for example, effectively discusses some of the persistent ethnic conflicts continuing to plague Brazil, India, and the United States while presenting extensive evidence diminishing the significance of ethnic factors in the collapse of the USSR and Yugoslavia. Hao (2012), however, has also expressed personal admiration for America's "melting pot" formula, which helped to forge its strong national identity. But Hao does stress that China's situation, as a non-immigrant country, is different. Not opposed to all aspects of the reformist critique, Hao agrees that the removal of *minzu* categories from identification cards might help eliminate some cases of ethnic discrimination. In general, however, Hao Shiyuan backs the status quo, arguing that current policies are working and should be retained.

Other individuals within the *minzu* establishment, especially younger Han and minority scholars, question some aspects of current policy. A number of them have privately expressed sympathy with some aspects of the reform agenda with the author. Some are openly critical of the way the current system hinders the development of shared interactions, understandings, and a collective sense of belonging.

Yet many of these younger scholars are also concerned about the implications of any policy shifts, especially if they are reactive and poorly managed. They argue that the reforms advocated by Hu Angang and Hu Lianhe would only intensify, rather than alleviate, ethnic tensions and conflicts. This is a particular concern when one considers China's authoritarian political culture, demographic/spatial imbalance, and weak legal system.

These younger scholars tend to speak of the need to perfect (完善) rather than readjust (调整) current policies. They also propose a range of new initiatives they argue would be more prudent. Such initiatives include increased interethnic dialogue and mediation, encouraging hyphenated ethnic identifications (such as Tibetan-Chinese), expansion of civic and intercultural education, mandated bilingualism for all Han cadres in ethnic regions, and an experimental bottom-up form of ethnic autonomy giving real authority to local officials (See Jia, Lee, and Zhang 2012; Carlson 2009; Guan 2007: 279–323).

In recent years this debate has become increasingly public. Prior to 2008, Ma Rong's ideas were generally addressed in abstract and detached discussions in largely obscure academic books and journals (*cf.* Hao 2005; Sautman 2010: 79). Today Ma's views are part of the mainstream conversation concerning options for ethnic-policy reform as addressed in leading newspapers, party journals, and websites.[6]

Over five million party members and additional millions more are employed in positions tied to the ethnic status quo

The size of the *minzu* establishment is vast. Over five million party members and additional millions more are employed in positions directly or indirectly tied to the ethnic status quo. This ensures a vigorous defense of current policy, if not policy inertia.

Some have spoken of ethnic cadres as a new aristocratic stratum (新贵阶层) in frontier regions such as Tibet. These party officials are fundamentally detached from their ethnic communities and are dependent on the CPC and its current ethnic system (Gongmen Law Research Center 2009).

"These officials," Tibetan blogger Tsering Woeser notes, "are all eating *minzu* rice. If ethnic policies are adjusted or changed, this will have a big impact on their interests and thus they will attempt to block any adjustment to ethnic policies" (cited in Ye B. 2009).

Gauging Public Opinion: Right, Left, and Center

What does the wider intellectual and policy community in China, especially those citizen intellectuals outside the *minzu* establishment, make of the ethnic-policy reform agenda? Barry Sautman argues that proposals to "curb minority rights" "emanate from a small number of Chinese academics" yet "reflect a prominent strand of thinking about ethnic policies" (Sautman 2010: 72; 2012: 26). Despite these observations, Sautman detected in early 2012 a "subtle shift" in policy following the recent unrest, with signs of a more populist and pragmatic approach to "improving people's livelihood" in frontier regions like Tibet and Xinjiang.

There is no lack of speculation in the Western and overseas Chinese media regarding how new CPC Secretary General Xi Jinping will handle ethnic issues. Based on his father's supposedly close relationship with the Dalai Lama and rumors that his wife is a devout disciple of Tibetan Buddhism, some have suggested that Xi "may adopt a more reformist approach" and follow his father in "championing the rights of Tibetans, Uighurs, and other ethnic minorities" (Lim and Daniel, 2012; *cf.* M. Liu 2012; Hong 2012).

Similarly, leading Tibet specialist Robert Barnett remains cautiously optimistic that "a softer approach" on Tibet could emerge under the new leadership (Schiavenza 2013). Barnett has long argued that Tibet policy, at least, is a "bargaining chip" in factional politics which may be played at any time (M. Liu 2012).

There are unconfirmed reports that local officials in Qinghai (and perhaps Sichuan province) are easing the denunciation of the Dalai Lama in some Tibetan monasteries (RFA 2013; ICT 2013). If true, this would suggest a willingness on behalf of the regime to try new approaches. But it's unclear at this stage whether these sorts of changes are harbingers of a more moderate policy or experimentation with new methods for stabilizing and controlling Tibetan regions that have witnessed high rates of self-immolation.

As the following commentary seeks to demonstrate, high-level opinion does not indicate a softening when it comes to ethnic unity, and there appears to be little public support for greater minority rights and autonomy. Rather, opinion seems to be moving in the opposite direction, with growing talk of the need to increase interethnic cohesion and fusion while adopting policies that strengthen a shared sense of Chinese identity instead of narrow ethnic consciousness. This sentiment crosses ethnic and ideological lines and increases the likelihood of eventual policy adjustments in this direction.

On many key issues, critical opinion remains divided between right and left positions—with liberals favoring a further dismantling of state controls in favor of free-market mechanisms while those on the left believe a strong state is required in a country as large and complex as China. Both share, however, a similar crisis mentality (忧患意识)—the sort of "nation-centered" "patriotic worrying" that Gloria Davies (2007: 15–57) argues transcends ideological divisions.

In fact, as discussed below, citizen intellectuals of various ideologies are increasingly concerned over the implications of current ethnic tension for China's ongoing revival and territorial integrity.

The Chinese Liberals

As was the case ten years ago, Chinese liberals have lofty hopes for the party's so-called fifth generation of leaders under Xi Jinping. With Bo Xilai purged and the left in disarray, liberals hope Xi's administration will reignite the flames of economic reform and, perhaps, even loosen political controls. However, the implications for possible reform of ethnic policy remain equivocal. The diversity within the "liberal camp" now includes voices sharply critical of current ethnic policies. But, as yet, there is no agreement on the best solution for current problems.

Blame for current problems is, however, consistently assigned to China's autocratic and conservative political system. Ethnic concerns are often viewed as peripheral and dependent on solutions for the larger issue of political legitimacy. Chinese liberals tend to assume that ethnic tensions will end or gradually diminish only when "China proper" moves toward a more representative democratic political system.

Democratization, Liu Xiaobo (2012: 262–6) wrote after the 3/14 Incident, is a precondition for any solution to the Tibet problem: "So long as people in China proper are denied authentic self-rule, self-rule for Tibetans and other minorities will remain a pipe dream."

Other liberals fear that, without increased ethnic and cultural cohesiveness, greater democracy could lead to national dissolution. Tracing liberal thought over the last decade identifies a significant shift in opinion. Some prominent liberals now back the sort of reforms advocated by Ma Rong and Hu Angang while others have either softened or qualified their previous support for minority rights in the wake of recent ethnic violence.

Some prominent liberals now back the sort of reforms advocated by Ma Rong and Hu Angang

One example would be the "Charter 08 Movement," which Feng Chongyi (2010) identifies as "the apotheosis of the Chinese liberal

camp" and "an embodiment and synthesis of theoretical and intellectual achievements by Chinese liberal intellectuals over a decade."
This bold December 10, 2008, manifesto for reform, signed by 303
concerned individuals, had its origins in the 1996 October Tenth
Declaration. In the earlier declaration, Wang Xizhe and Liu Xiaobo
(1996) spoke of the universal "right of minorities to self-determination," and highlighted that during the Jiangxi Soviet (1931–34) "self-
determination" had been interpreted by the CPC as the right of small
ethnic groups to break away and form their own independent states.

Yet Charter 08 makes no mention of self-determination. Its second-
to-the-last goal states: "We should approach disputes in the national
minority areas of China with an open mind, seeking to find a workable
framework within which all ethnic and religious groups can flourish.
We should aim ultimately at a federation of democratic communities
of China" (Link 2009). Here neither the specific form nor the scope
of this federation are specified (many interpreted it as only addressing
Hong Kong, Macau, and Taiwan), leaving the status of Tibet, Xinjiang, and other minority regions unclear (Guo 2009). This reflects
the lack of consensus on ethnic issues, if not open disagreement. Charter 08 was issued after the Lhasa riots and before the Ürümqi riots,
events that led many of its signatories to call for policy reform aimed
at safeguarding national unity and interethnic cohesion.

Prominent liberal blogger Ran Yunfei, for example, is a member of
the Tujia minority from Sichuan province who spent years working
among minority communities in the highlands of Western Sichuan.
His activism saw him detained for six months in March 2011, and
cemented his online celebrity status on microblog platforms Weibo
and Twitter (Johnson 2012b). Despite his clearly liberal orientation,
in a post-3/14 essay Ran (2008) is hardly sympathetic to minority
concerns. Acknowledging that "appeals for ethnic, religious and human rights are extremely thorny issues," Ran condemns the violence
directed at Han citizens (which he compares to terrorist acts and Pales-
tinian suicide bombers) and argues that the government cannot afford
to be too conciliatory.

Despite his signing Charter 08 later that year, in this earlier essay
Ran makes no mention of federalism and proposes instead "a high
degree of genuine autonomy for Tibet under a condition of political
unity." Then, following the 7/5 riots, his views seemed to harden

further. In a July 2009 blog post, Ran Yunfei writes that ethnic autonomy is no longer possible under the CPC's totalitarian and despotic rule. He is highly critical of the fossilized and conservative nature of the CPC's ethnic policies. He blames these policies for the "tragic, large-scale massacre" in Ürümqi. To replace the current "divide and rule" approach which only "strengthens ethnic identity," Ran calls for China to follow the US model where all individuals (regardless of their ethnic identity) are treated, at least theoretically, as equals before the law (Ran 2009).

Ran's views reflect widespread concerns regarding the implications of democracy on national unity. Prominent liberal Deng Yuwen, who was recently dismissed from his post as senior deputy editor of *Study Times*, argued in 2012 that any rash, premature, move toward universal suffrage could split the nation along its ethnic seams—meaning further ethnic stitching is a prerequisite for any political reform (Deng 2012). "Within the inner-most soul of the Chinese people," Hong Kong-based intellectual Wang Shaoguang (2002: 53) wrote, "there exists an extraordinary fear of state dismemberment."

Liu Junning, another signatory of Charter 08, has long advocated a federalist solution. In 2002 he wrote: "Regardless of its economy, China possesses a marked diversity in terms of social cultures and thus should naturally be a federated state" (Liu J. 2002). Yet, like many other liberals, ethnic clashes caused him to either rethink or clarify his position.

Liu claims that the CPC's Soviet-derived policies depart from both Chinese tradition and international norms and thus must go

A self-styled "classical liberal," Liu is a champion of the universality of individual rights and was forced out of CASS because of his outspoken political views (Liu J. 2000; 2011). Several days after the Ürümqi riots, Liu (2009) argued that genuine political autonomy must be built on a foundation of ethnic unity. Instead of dissolving and mitigating ethnic contradictions, Liu stated, minority affirmative action and regional ethnic autonomy have exacerbated ethnic divisions and will only lead to further ethnic conflict. By creating legal distinctions between *minzu* groups, Liu claims, the CPC's Soviet-derived policies depart from both Chinese tradition and international norms and thus must go.

In a bold fashion, he concludes:

Thus, so that people of all ethnic groups can co-exist and co-fuse
across China, we should abolish the concept of 'minzu' both
politically and legally. To eliminate the differences between ethnic identities, we should scrap the minzu category on residency,
identification, and dossier files; abolish the different ways of referring to the nation and the ethnic minorities; and, instead,
render everyone equal by giving the people of each ethnic group
the right to retain and defend their cultural traditions (Ibid).

In a conversation with journalist Xiao Sanza (2012), Liu declared
that "the policy of regional ethnic autonomy is a disguised form of
ethnic segregation" that should be abolished to pave the way for a
territorial, rather than ethnic-based, model of federalism like that of
the United States.

Similarly the prominent liberal intellectual Li Datong (2009b), the
former editor of *China Youth Daily*'s controversial *Freezing Point* (冰
点) magazine, called on China to "free itself from the trap" of the
CPC's current ethnic policies. On the website of the BBC's Chinese
language service, he claimed "the root cause of all ethnic problems
today is the way we emphasize and strengthen ethnic differences."

Like Liu, Li Datong was dismissed from his post in 2006 for criti-
cizing government censorship and eventually signed Charter 08; yet
his views in this 2009 essay show the marked influence of Ma Rong
(Hu 2009). By trying to solve ethnic issues in Tibet or Inner Mongol through political autonomy, the CPC "is slavishly following the
USSR" and adopting cultural strategies completely alien from Chinese
tradition. The result is the identification and, in some cases, the out-
right creation, of fifty-six *minzu* groups that depart from the Republic
of Five Races (五族共和) that maintained harmonious ethnic relations during the Republican period (Li D. 2009b; 2011).

"This creation and strengthening of national differences," Li Datong
(2009a) wrote in English on *Open Democracy*, "meant that members of
minority nationalities came to identify more with their ethnicity than
their country." Like other reformers, Li (2009b) praises the US-style
"melting pot" which helped to produce the first African-American president of the United States—Barack Obama. "For over a half a century,

China has carried out this system of minority autonomy, yet which Tibetan, Mongol, Uyghur, or Hui individual has been able to assume the position of Secretary General of the CPC or Chinese president?"

Among Chinese liberals, Tsinghua University historian and public intellectual Qin Hui has perhaps the most nuanced views on ethnic issues. While he decided against signing Charter 08, he remains a stalwart supporter of a federalist, democratic solution to China's problems. Yet like Liu Junning, he envisions a US-style union rather than the failed USSR model. In a 2008 dialogue with left intellectuals, Qin Hui stated unequivocally: "I believe in the future China will be a unified state but also a federalist state" (Wang Y. 2008).

In December 2011 Qin Hui expanded on his views in light of the then-recent violence in Xinjiang and Tibet (Cao 2012). Admitting there are "some serious problems with the Leninist-system of ethnic autonomy" and "the current situation is getting worse," he seemed to struggle with the implications of a democratizing China for ethnic relations, admitting that ethnic hatred and the potential for ethnic maniacs (民族狂人) pose serious threats to democracy in large, heterogeneous countries such as China. "Of course," he is reported to have stated, "I believe that ethnic unity is important but there are actually big problems with the way we are currently handling ethnic unity."

Late last year Qin Hui appeared to arrive at a solution to this dilemma. In an article reflecting on the place of ethnicity in the former Yugoslavia and in contemporary Indian society, Qin (2012) advocates what he termed left-right pluralism (左右多元化). As he explains, both of these countries are the product of foreign colonialism and adopted a federalist state structure. Yet their contrasting political cultures (Leninism in Yugoslavia versus constitutional democracy in India) led to divergent outcomes: the dissolution of the former and increased economic and political

Elections in countries like India and the United States, Qin Hui argues, function as 'great baptisms of ethnic fusion'

vibrancy in the latter. Tito's "forced ethnic pluralism" crumbled on his death while India's colorful democracy has overcome ethnic and religions differences by making ideology, instead of identity, the focus of Indian politics.

Elections in countries like India and the United States, Qin Hui argues, function as "great baptisms of ethnic fusion" with different political parties forced to appeal to voters across ethnic and religious spectrums. For Qin Hui, this sort of left-right competition guards against national disintegration because: 1) ideological positions, unlike ethnocultural identities, are changeable personal choices; 2) small political parties, unlike ethnic minority communities, can be transformed into large, mainstream organizations; and 3) political divisions are rational and reasonably justified when contrasted with the emotionalism of ethnic identities. Without making any specific recommendations for China, Qin Hui concludes that left-right pluralism is the best defense against ethnic polarization and state fragmentation in multiethnic countries.

The influential Beijing-based couple Wang Lixiong and his half-Tibetan wife Tsering Woeser have a similarly nuanced yet conflicted view of ethnic politics in China. Both are fierce critics of the CPC and its current policies, advocating robust protection of the Tibetan language, religion, and way of life.

Like his wife, Wang Lixiong (2008a; 2008b) points to the "Chinesization of Tibet" as the "root cause" of the current conflict and claims the financial resources with which the CPC has attempted to address problems in Tibet have failed to win the hearts and minds of the Tibetan people. He speaks of a "rigid, inflexible, and hard-line" bureaucracy "pushing China toward the abyss of split." The best and most practical solution, in Wang's opinion, is "progressive democracy." This would be gradual democratic reform rooted in village elections that would both "guarantee China's sovereignty and let Tibet achieve 'high autonomy'." Rather than self-immolating, Tibetans should follow their fellow citizens in Wukan, Guangdong, in demanding village autonomy (Wang L. 2012).

Woeser has expressed concerns about the growing traction of Ma Rong's ideas among liberals and fears that the removal of regional ethnic autonomy would be the death knell for Tibetan culture and identity (Carlson 2009).

Yet, like many other Chinese intellectuals, there is an identifiable tension in the writings of Wang and Woeser between the desire to preserve minority cultures and the need to break down the policy "moats" segregating Tibetans and other minorities from mainstream Chinese society. Woeser says Chinese political controls in Tibet resemble South African apartheid or the isolation of the Gaza Strip (Woeser 2012). The state's *minzu*-based preferences act as yet another barrier and thus should be scrapped, according to Woeser (Ford 2012).

The Chinese Left and Ultra-Nationalists

One finds similar dissatisfaction with current ethnic policies on the left side of Chinese politics. Like their liberal colleagues, the so-called New Left (新左派) is defined more by political orientation than any single, coherent, or homogeneous policy agenda. Rooted in the post-1989 defense of the Chinese revolution and indigenous tradition, the Chinese left favors a neo-statist approach to public policy containing an, at times, eclectic mix of popular nationalism, social justice, and a predilection for indigenous solutions to contemporary problems.

Even more than their liberal colleagues, the left places a premium on national unity and remaining vigilant against internal and external forces seeking to tear the nation asunder. Because China's ethnic groups have lived intermingled for centuries and share common origins, the left rejects federalism as ill-suited for China.

In the words of prominent New Left economist Wen Tiejun, federalism would be suicidal and would sever the coastal provinces from the oil, water, and other natural resources necessary for China's continued rise (Wang Y. 2008).

Market reform has exacerbated social divisions, most on the left agree, causing class and regional differences to be "ethnicized" and requiring strong state management to control long-standing ethnic tensions. Many on the left are openly nostalgic for the socialist past where, they believe, a shared political ideology united different ethnic communities under the leadership of Chairman Mao.

Although he rejects the label, many view Wang Hui as the New Left's leading voice. Currently a professor of Chinese language and literature at Tsinghua University, Wang edited the prominent magazine *Readings* (读书) for over ten years and regularly appears on lists of the most influential intellectuals in China.

Like many other citizen intellectuals, Wang began questioning current ethnic policies in the wake of the 3/14 Incident. In a long, highly discursive, essay (which first appeared as an interview transcript in

2008 before being extensively revised) published in English in 2011, Wang renews (in the fashion of Edward Said) the frontal attack on Western Orientalism. Wang expresses particular venom for the West's misguided fantasies about Tibet. He blames a "Shangri-la effect" for the distorted coverage of the Lhasa riots in Western media and speaks of a more general Western tendency to overlook the dramatic economic, political, and social improvements occurring inside Tibet since 1949 (Wang Hui 2011: 137–54).

Wang warns of locking in ethnic differences through state classifications and restrictions on mobility

Like many of his colleagues, Wang Hui believes ethnic tensions are rising in China. He speaks of a "crisis of legitimacy" in Tibet and, more broadly, throughout China and warns of locking in ethnic differences through state classifications and restrictions on mobility. He addresses the danger that the current system of local autonomy "will calcify, become conservative, and turn into a merely top-down order of social control and management" (Wang Hui 2011: 195).

"Economic integration has not spawned a sense of social integration," Wang writes, "but rather given rise to a sense of social division" (Wang Hui 2011: 207–8). Referring to Ma Rong's writing as "most incisive and profound," Wang Hui agrees that current ethnic policies need to be "adjusted" but rejects calls for wholesale system redesign. Current policies, he argues, are not only "the culmination of the Chinese historical tradition and the experience of the revolution" (Ibid. 195) but also the best method for achieving "actual equality" rather then simply legal equality at a statutory level.

In sharp contrast to Ma Rong, however, Wang Hui blames current problems on the "de-politicization" of ethnic affairs. The developmental logic of the market is incapable of ameliorating social and ethnic contradictions, he contends. Instead, a new "politics of recognition" and "politics of dignity" are required. The state must actively balance unity and diversity by placing a premium on social diversity (namely "unity in diversity"), recognizing group-differentiated rights, and fostering a "new society based on universal equality" (Ibid. 197).

In suggesting policy adjustments, Wang Hui follows Wang Lixiong and other liberals in calling for "smaller scale" "grassroots" autonomy

(Ibid. 191) but struggles to clearly define the precise balance between unity and diversity in the Chinese context. Perhaps the best example of this tension is his convoluted discussion of language as it relates to Tibetan identity (Ibid. 215–7), where he cites fellow progressive Hobsbawm on the inevitability of some languages disappearing. "So, on the one hand you want minorities to study their own language and preserve their distinctiveness," he told a Western journalist, "but you don't want that difference to result in even greater social inequality. We must protect minority cultures, but also make sure they have access to the means of upward mobility" (Wang Hui 2008: 12–13).

In the wake of the 3/14 Incident, Cui Zhiyuan (2009), Wang Hui's New Left colleague at Tsinghua University, argued that the sort of de-territorialized "national cultural autonomy" advocated by Austrian Social Democrats Otto Bauer and Karl Renner during the early twentieth century is a more effective method for protecting ethnocultural diversity and territorial and national unity in China. This approach would attenuate group rights and strengthen the domination of the ethnic majority, according to Barry Sautman (2010: 64).

Like the Chinese liberals, several prominent voices on the left have called for more fundamental changes to ethnic policies. Popular New Left websites such as Utopia (乌有之乡, www.wyzxsd.com) and Grassroots (草根, www.caogen.com) contain numerous posts highly critical of the current approach.

In a recently reposted article on Utopia, for example, policy adviser Mei Xinyu (2012) rebukes those inside the *minzu* system for uncritically resisting any reconsideration of existing ethnic policies: "We cannot attribute all of China's ethnic problems to a lack of sufficient economic development, rather we should evaluate the facts so that we can gradually perfect our policy." He points to the failure of economic development in stemming ethnic violence in the Niger Delta and Sudan. However, like Wang Hui, Mei stops short of advocating wholesale change. Unlike Wang, Mei is highly critical of *minzu*-based preferences, claiming they violate the principle of equality and do not encourage a spirit of self-struggle.

On Grassroots, popular Phoenix television commentator Qiu Zhenghai (2009) argues that rising ethnic tensions could lead to China's "Waterloo movement," and tip the nation into disintegration. Frequent *United Morning Daily* (联合早报) commentator Yu Shiyu

(2009) blames "Beijing's fossilized and short-sighted ethnic policies" for growing ethnic estrangement and calls for a strengthening of national identification and social interchange between ethnic groups. Finally, Yi Fuxian (2009), one of China's leading critics of the one-child policy, calls for a scrapping of regional ethnic autonomy. Yi argues that this Stalinist policy "artificially created new ethnic groups" and caused those identified as minority populations in Western Hunan, for example, to increase from 6.4 percent in 1949 to nearly 40 percent today.

Sima Pingbang (2009a; 2009b) is another prominent and outspoken New Left blogger. In several posts following the 7/5 Incident, he attacked ethnic-based preferences. For him, the poorly understood nature of these unjust policies explains why most foreigners misinterpret the Ürümqi tragedy. Rather than oppressing the Uyghurs, as many foreigners believe, the government's appeasement policies emboldened them and thus sparked the violence in Xinjiang. These preferences, Sima argues, weaken national cohesion and violate the core principle of human rights—that all men are born equal. An optimist, he concludes that within a hundred or so years the very idea of fifty-six distinct ethnic groups will disappear—with different groups following their ancestors in fusing together into a cohesive whole.

Among more radical voices on the left, what some call the extreme left (及左派), there are also those who are critical of the current Chinese approach to ethnic contradictions. The solution for Kong Qingdong

'We must do some soul searching about our ethnic policies, awake from our coma, and strengthen unity'

and other neo-Maoists is simple: return to the socialist past. Mao correctly identified ethnic tensions as stemming from class contradictions, they argue, and the government must rely on the masses, as opposed to a small stratum of nobles and monks, to solve the Tibet problem. Speaking on his popular Internet-television show following "the sixtieth anniversary of the peaceful liberation of Tibet," Kong declared: "In the hearts and minds of the Tibetan people, Chairman Mao is the most respected living Buddha" (Kong Q. 2011a). With regards to Xinjiang, he goes on to state:

We must do some soul searching about our ethnic policies, awake from our coma, and strengthen unity. This is the best policy for eliminating terrorist organizations. If you don't grasp popular sentiment, manage relations between officials and the people, and unify ethnic groups, it doesn't matter how much money or troops you throw at the problem, you won't be able to effect a fundamental solution to the problem.

If the "poison" of ethnic contradictions cannot be expelled, Kong wrote in another context, the mahjong tiles will tumble quickly and China will suddenly find itself with Sichuan and Sha'anxi as new border regions (Kong Q. 2011b).

Wang Xiaodong (2007; 2009), who was at the forefront of the ultra-nationalist publications *China Can Say No* (中国可以说不) and *Unhappy China* (中国不高兴), is equally critical of the government's current approach. During a series of online chats with pro-Han activists on Hanwang (汉网, www.hanminzu.org), Wang expressed sympathy with their criticism of minority preferences and support for the promotion of Han identity—but also called for unity and an increased spirit of militarism in the face of foreign interference in Tibet and Xinjiang.

Lastly, high-profile international-relations expert Yan Xuetong (2009) recently identified national cohesion as one of the biggest challenges facing China's re-emergence on the global stage. Yan is currently the director of the Institute of International Studies at Tsinghua University and editor of the influential *Chinese Journal of International Politics* (国际政治科学). Yan has a PhD from the University of California, Berkeley, and, while he is principally a nationalist, has been described as "a Chinese-style neo-con" by some in the West and as a modern-day Confucius by others.

Without a clear "guiding principle" on the structure and fabric of the Chinese nation, Yan told a reporter in 2009, the West easily criticizes China for destroying ethnic diversity while continuing its own integrationist strategies such as insisting on a single national language. "The contradictions within our policy," he elaborates, "cause serious hindrance to the process of national integration." Yan mentions, as examples, the existence of multiple currencies (mainland China, Hong Kong, Macau, and Taiwan) and the household-registration system that "restricts the freedom of movement among the masses and slows the rate of co-residency among different ethnic groups." He further argues that, when faced with the current international environment—one that favors national disintegration and new states over the status quo—these sort of policies not only strengthen regional and ethnic identities that compete with a shared national identity but also pose a real danger to China's rise. Today's new conditions compel China to "go a step further in adjusting and perfecting our [ethnic] policies" (Yan 2009).

Broader Public Opinion

How thoroughly does the sentiment for ethnic-policy reform permeate Chinese society? Public opinion is notoriously difficult to ascertain in China, especially on issues as sensitive as ethnic policies and relations. The Internet, however, has created new platforms for articulating popular enthusiasms outside the confines of the carefully controlled state media. With over half-a-billion users, the Chinese language Internet has emerged as a popular vehicle for Chinese "netizens" to express their ideas. Interactive platforms, including blogs, bulletin-board systems, and microblogs, displaying a diversity of viewpoints (as well as those of commenters) is one of the defining features of the Internet in China. Not surprisingly, one can find a broad range of views on ethnic issues publicly posted.

The rise of Han chauvinism on the Sinophone Internet has earlier been documented (Leibold 2010a; 2010b). Groups of Han netizens (concentrated on the Chinese mainland but including others from around the globe) have become vocal critics of the CPC's ethnic policies. Retired Chinese government officials and struggling entrepreneurs join academics and university students in attacking minority preferences for undermining Han power and prestige. Many Han supremacists openly advocate a new round of assimilation to restore the "natural ethnic order."

'Using preferential treatment for minorities to achieve harmony is like giving kids candies to keep them happy'

Online criticism of current Chinese ethnic policies goes far beyond Han chauvinists, however. There is also a visible rise of more mainstream, so-called angry youth (*fenqing* 愤青), nationalism that views ethnic divisions as a source of national weakness (Osnos 2008). Following the 3/14 Incident, *fenqing* youth criticized not only Western reporting and perceptions on Tibet and other frontier regions but also their own government's policy of "minority appeasement." As one overseas-based youth put it: "Using preferential treatment for minorities to achieve harmony is like giving kids candies to keep them happy. One day, kids will grow up and blame their parents for rotting their teeth" (Berlinf 2009).

One can find a range of views—some explicitly critical of current ethnic policies and others strongly supportive—on mainstream platforms such as Baidu Post Bar (百度贴吧, http://tieba.baidu.com), QQ Forum (QQ论坛, http://bbs.qq.com), and even the *People's Daily's* Strong Nation Forum (强国社区, http://bbs1.people.com.cn). Perhaps most surprising, however, criticism of the CPC's ethnic policies has crept into more "liberal" spheres of the Chinese language Internet such as Sina Weibo (新浪微博, www.weibo.com), the BBC's Chinese language service, and Chinese language posts on Twitter.

One recent example would be the flood of criticism and discussion concerning minority policy when, following a brawl with Han villagers, local authorities in central China reportedly compensated a group of Uyghur traders US$25,000 for some damaged nut cake (切糕). Tweets including "China's ethnic policies is [*sic*] the root of all its ethnic problems" and thousands of others claiming reverse discrimination were posted (Alia 2012; Ford 2012). In this situation Internet posts mirrored contemporary intellectual debates, the BBC's Meng Ke (2012) argued, but tended to be more one-sided and Han-centric given the relative scarcity of minority voices online.

Online polls provide another window into public opinion. While the sample size is small, in one poll over 82 percent of 3,214 Weibo users favored the elimination of preferential extra points (加分) on university entrance exams for minorities and other disadvantaged groups with only 9 percent agreeing that it is "quite reasonable" to extend this benefit to minority students.[7]

One must be, however, extremely cautious in drawing conclusions on the extent and influence of critical views on the Chinese language Internet. Numerous examples exist of netizens actively supporting current ethnic policies and even upholding the values of Western-style multiculturalism in China. The budding field of cybermetrics offers other, more empirical, tools for tracking public-opinion trends. Data obtained through Baidu Index (百度指数, http:// index.baidu.com), for example, clearly demonstrates increased public interest in ethnic policy (民族政策). This may be measured by Baidu statistics for user searches and media reports containing this term.[8] There has, in fact, been a dramatic increase in the term's usage in the aftermath of the 7/5 Incident.

One finds a similar spike in searches for and news about Ma Rong (马戎)[9] beginning in the middle of 2010 and peaking during the spring of 2012 when debate surrounding the proposed second generation of ethnic policies was at its height. There are similar trends for the terms fusion (融合) and autonomous region (自治区), which are often (although not exclusively) used alongside *minzu* (as in ethnic fusion [民族融合] and ethnic autonomous region [民族自治区]). There has also been a steady (albeit erratic) increase in web searches for the terms Chinese nation/race (中华民族) and ethnic/national unity (民族团结).

These search analytics demonstrate increased public discussion of and interest in ethnic issues but tell us little about actual opinion or influence. To what extent is public opinion on ethnic issues shaped by deeper cognitive frames? Since 1949 the party-state has attempted to instill the values of cultural diversity and multiethnic harmony through its education and propaganda systems and these efforts should not be underestimated. Still, as research by Dikötter (1992), Cheng Yinghong (2011), Callahan (2013), and others has demonstrated, Chinese society remains deeply racist and xenophobic.

For millennium the Han Chinese have viewed "outsiders" (both long-nosed foreigners and more familiar nomads) with suspicion and mistrust. Circumstances might mandate peaceful co-existence or segregation but the ultimate goal is voluntary transformation: the elimination of outsiders and any ethnocultural variance through sedentism, intermarriage, and the acceptance of Han norms.

"In practice, though not formally, the Han Chinese think of themselves overwhelmingly as a nation-race," wrote Martin Jacques (2009: 266). Liang Qichao and then Sun Yat-sen employed the neologism *guozu* (国族, literally "state-race") to signify this deeply composite and consanguineous self-identification. Interestingly, Hu Angang and Hu Lianhe resurrected this term in their call for a second generation of ethnic policies.

Direction of Ethnic Policy under Xi Jinping

What do China's top leaders think about ethnic-policy reform? The short answer is that very little is actually known about leadership attitudes on this issue. Barry Sautman (2010; 2012: 26) recently wrote that the debate over ethnic policies has reached the top levels of the CPC but, in his estimation, "present indications are that the government intends to basically maintain existing policies." The last year, however, produced some interesting developments—including a once-in-a-decade leadership transition ushering in a new generation of CPC leaders under new Secretary General Xi Jinping.

What can be expected for ethnic policy under Xi? Will, as many inside and outside China hope, his rule bring a new approach to ethnic policy? If so, in which direction? There are certainly signs that some within the top CPC leadership are openly sympathetic to the ideas of Ma Rong, Hu Angang, and other policy reformers—although we only have fragmented pieces of information at this stage.

Zhu Weiqun's "Personal Opinion"

In February 2012 the then executive director of the UFWD, the party's top organ for overseeing ethnic policy, made a rare personal appeal for rethinking some aspects of current ethnic policy. In the lead article in *Study Times,* Zhu Weiqun (2012) admitted some serious problems with the current approach and, like many other reformers, waved the specter of a disintegrated and blood-torn USSR and Yugoslavia before his readers. He argued that the current focus on state-guided development will not solve ethnic problems and, instead, called for more emphasis on voluntary, self-initiated ethnic mingling and fusion (民族交融融合). The CPC should not allow administrative measures to hinder the free flow of people or allow ethnic differences to calcify, Zhu asserted.

As a concrete example of what the party-state could do along these lines, Zhu personally recommended the removal of ethnic status from identification cards, a freeze on any new ethnic autonomous units, ethnically mixed schooling, and the strengthening of Putonghua education. As Zhu has been, since 2006, one of the party's chief spokesmen on ethnic and religious affairs and its key interlocutor in talks with representatives of the Dalai Lama, his article attracted widespread attention in academic, media, and policy circles and has been widely reposted across the Chinese language Internet.

Zhu Weiqun's ideas clearly have much in common with those presented by Ma Rong and Hu Angang. Neither of these two individuals is mentioned by name in Zhu's article but Ma Rong has earlier been identified (by an official at the US Embassy in Beijing) as a "frequent advisor" to the UFWD (Carlson 2009).

Following the publication of Zhu's article, the PRC's parallel administrative body for ethnic affairs, the State Ethnic Affairs Commission (SEAC), created a special "Probing a Second Generation of Ethnic Policies" webpage on its main propaganda portal (中国民族宗教网, www.mzb.com.cn). A prominent banner on the homepage served to draw readers' attention to the "battle of opinions" webpage where a collection of articles debating Hu Angang's proposal were housed.[10]

While the site contains more than twenty articles by Hao Shiyuan and others attacking the reform agenda, and only a handful in support, the very public display of this policy disagreement on a state-managed website is unprecedented and seems to reflect similar divisions at the top reaches of the CPC. This possibly indicates a degree of tension or disagreement between the state (SEAC) bureaucracy and the party (UFWD) bureaucracy when it comes to ethnic policy.

> *This policy disagreement on a state-managed website is unprecedented and seems to reflect similar divisions at the top reaches of the CPC*

Outside the Chinese mainland, commentators have widely interpreted Zhu's article as a portent of eventual policy change. One anonymous source on the US-based Duowei News blog asserts: "…these opinions [for reform] are already ripe within the highest reaches of the CPC. To the extent that a common understanding has been reached, it is quite possible that this article reflects the CPC's habit of 'guiding public opinion' or sounding out the wider environment, although the call for reforming ethnic policy has long been heard" (Kong X. 2012).

In a March 2012 cover story, Hong Kong's popular *Phoenix Weekly* (凤凰周刊) hailed Zhu's article as a "breakthrough" in ethnic theory and suggested that it reflects the future direction of state policy (*Phoenix Weekly* 2012). He Liangliang (2012), one of the key political analysts on the Phoenix Satellite Television Network, told his audience that the reform agenda goes well beyond Zhu Weiqun and is no longer a mere academic debate. The fact that Zhu's article was published in *Study Times,* the official magazine of the Central Party School in Beijing, suggests the "imprimatur of the government," he asserted, and "by putting forward these thoughts, it signifies that China is currently preparing [for policy change]." "I believe," he added, "that reforms to ethnic policy are brewing."

Unlike He Liangliang, who openly sympathizes with the reform agenda, US-based dissident journalist Hu Ping (2012) arrived at a similar conclusion despite his strong criticisms of Ma Rong. Given Zhu Weiqun's long-standing role in shaping ethnic policy, Hu Ping believes "the article reflects, to a large extent, the policy direction of the Chinese government regarding minority affairs and deserves to be studied closely."

In reaction to the article, some CPC officials have publicly distanced themselves from Zhu's remarks. Former Tibetan Autonomous Region (TAR) Chairman Qiangba Puncog denied that Zhu's comments signal the need for a policy reversal. When questioned by a reporter, Qiangba stated: "Our party's ethnic policies have been extremely successful" (Chen 2012).

Still, the simple fact that Chinese reporters on the mainland are now actively querying top CPC officials on the direction of ethnic policy reflects the increased openness and prominence of this debate (*cf.* Li and Wang 2012).

Hu Jintao's Legacy and Personnel Changes

Despite the clamor for ethnic-policy change, significant institutional and political barriers render such changes unlikely in the immediate future. As is the case with broader efforts aimed at political and economic reform in China, deeply entrenched bureaucratic and patronage-based interests makes significant policy changes extremely difficult. This may be evidenced by the failure to alter largely unpopular national family planning (计划生育), re-education through labor (劳教), and household-registration (户籍) policies.

Moreover, current ethnic policies are closely associated with the legacy of former Secretary General Hu Jintao. As TAR party-secretary from 1988–92, Hu Jintao played a direct rule in coordinating ethnic policy during his ten-year tenure at the top. Hu personally identified the "correct handling of ethnic issues" as "an important criterion for judging the ability of the CPC to govern and the capacity of party organizations to lead" (Leading Group of the SEAC 2012). Any radical or sudden shift in policy would be viewed as a repudiation of Hu Jintao's legacy and the policies of his mentor Hu Yaobang, the chief architect of post-Mao ethnic policies and also a key supporter of Xi Jinping's political rise. Recent administrative appointments also suggest that Hu Jintao's ethnic-policy legacy is likely to be carefully guarded for at least the near future.

Following his rather spectacular fall from grace (after his son's embarrassing death in a Ferrari car crash), Ling Jihua, one of Hu Jintao's closest aides, was appointed as the new head of the UFWD in August 2012. Ling, who previously led the General Office of the CPC's Central Committee, was once a leading candidate for the PBSC. However, during the recent Eighteenth Party Congress, Ling was not even appointed to the politburo (Johnson 2012a). While Ling's political influence has clearly been diminished, he remains in a powerful position regarding the continuation or change of ethnic policy.

Zhu Weiqun's current successor as the day-to-day director of the UFWD, Zhang Yijiong, is another Hu Jintao ally. Unlike the princeling (太子党) Zhu Weiqun, Zhang is closely associated with Hu Jintao's *tuanpai* faction (团派, Youth League faction). Zhang has spent most of his career, including a recent posting as the deputy party secretary of the TAR, as an official in Tibetan regions (TIN 2012).

Interestingly, the sixty-six-year-old Zhu Weiqun, who has yet to reach the mandatory retirement age, appears to have been pushed sideways. He failed to retain his seat on the Central Committee at the Eighteenth Party Congress, and in March 2013 was moved out of the UFWD and appointed director of the Ethnic and Religious Affairs Committee for the largely ceremonial Chinese People's Political Consultative Conference (CPPCC), a far less powerful position.

Following the Eighteenth Party Congress, it had been suggested that the locus of ethnic policy might shift to the recently expanded seven-man Secretariat of the Central Committee (Choi and Lau 2012; Wang Xin 2012). The secretariat is responsible for managing the day-to-day work of the politburo and the PBSC and, at times in the past, has played a significant role in policymaking.

Headed by PBSC member Liu Yunshan, who spent the first twenty years of his career in Inner Mongolia, the new secretariat now also includes two new appointees with extensive experience on ethnic policy: the outgoing director of the UFWD, Du Qinglin, and the former director of the SEAC, Yang Jing (now the most senior non-Han official in the CPC). As all three of these men are generally associated with the *tuanpai* faction and owe their career elevations to Hu Jintao, their appointments would seem to suggest that any change in ethnic policy is unlikely to come from this current body.

Yang Jing's elevation to secretary-general of the State Council in March 2013 now places him near the apex of decision-making within both the party and state bureaucracies. It is, however, unlikely that Yang or Wang Zhengwei, his successor at the SEAC, will exert definitive influence over the direction of ethnic policy under Xi Jinping (SCMP 2013; Chan 2013).

In fact, the individual that is emerging as the party's new point man on ethnic issues is PBSC member and Chair of the CPPCC Yu Zhengsheng, who was recently appointed head of the party's Central Leading Small Group (CLSG) on Tibet and Xinjiang (Choi 2013). In the past, the CLSG has taken a key coordinating and decision-making role on ethnic policy in the two regions, working closely with the UFWD, the SEAC, and party and security officials in the two regions while reporting directly to the PBSC. Before his recent promotion, the princeling Yu Zhengsheng spent several years as party secretary of Shanghai and is known to be close to former Secretary-General Jiang Zemin.

The continued influence of Jiang Zemin over party policy might favor long-term ethnic-policy reform, especially as his protégé Xi Jinping consolidates his power. The 87-year-old Jiang wielded significant influence over the make up of the current politburo and PBSC, with four of the seven PBSC members identified as part of his Shanghai-based patronage network. There are reasons to believe that the "elite/princeling faction" of Jiang and Xi is more inclined toward ethnic-policy reform than Hu Jintao's "populist/ *tuanpai* faction."

Jiang reportedly clashed with Hu Jintao over ethnic policy following the 3/14 and 7/5 incidents. According to leading analyst Willy Lam (2009), Jiang Zemin attempted to convince the Central Military Commission and PBSC members that Hu's ethnic policies had failed in Xinjiang and Tibet and a new approach was required.

There are others in the top leadership who agree, including Hu Jin-tao's ally and new Vice Premier Wang Yang. Following the Shaoguan and Ürümqi violence, the then-Guangdong party secretary publicly appealed for adjustments in ethnic policies (Ye 2009). In the past, fellow politburo member and policy expert Wang Huning (2004: 365) asserted that "*minzu* fusion is an inevitable trend of history" and one that will eventually see "the complete elimination of ethnic differences, the withering away of *minzu*, and the fusion of all the world's nations." Wang offered these comments while director of the Central Committee's powerful Policy Research Center in a detailed exposition addressing the *minzu* question.

There are also signs that many within the security apparatuses would favor a new approach to ethnic policy (see Xu 2010). New initiatives from this direction would almost certainly favor increased national integration.

Outspoken General Liu Yazhou, one of the "princeling generals" with close ties to both Jiang Zemin and Xi Jinping, has long favored a new approach to ethnic affairs. Liu, who was recently promoted a full general, is currently the political commissar of the People's Liberation Army (PLA)'s National Defense University (NDU) in Beijing and a Central Committee member. Over a decade ago, Liu (2001) argued that China's future, in fact its "national destiny," lies in the west, especially Xinjiang and the Central Asian corridor (what Liu termed "the Euro-Asia land bridge"). Liu argued that this area was both home to the natural resources needed for China's continued rise and the weakest point in the US line of containment.

Solving long-standing religious and ethnic problems remains crucial to the success of Liu's "Go West" strategy. The threat of ethnic and religious separatism is an evident weakness to this plan. To counter this, Liu advocated breaking up both the TAR and the XUAR into smaller administrative bodies. He argued this action would attenuate separatist forces and ameliorate ethnic contradictions through a checks-and-balances system which would also generate more Han migration into these regions. Reform, Liu further argued, "is unavoidable" if China hoped to avoid the same fate as the USSR and Yugoslavia.

More recently, one of Liu's colleagues at NDU, Major General Xu Yan (2010) made an even more explicit call for policy reversal. In a *People's Daily* magazine he argued that "the weakening of specific ethnic identities is the most effective method for achieving inclusiveness" and, like others, contrasted the failed "ethnic coalitions" of the USSR and Yugoslavia with the melting-pot successes of India and the United States. "Both Chinese and Western history," Xu concludes, "proves that the best route for achieving ethnic unity is to promote mutual fusion of different ethnic groups under a condition of equality."

Xi's Chinese Dream and Ethnic Policy

Little is really known about what the man expected to lead China for the next decade thinks about ethnic policy. As evidenced by his keynote address at the ceremony in Lhasa celebrating "the sixtieth anniversary of the peaceful liberation of Tibet," Xi Jinping has, at least to date, carefully extolled the party line (Xinhua 2011a). He has had little direct experience with ethnic issues and would have to carefully navigate the conflicts of vested interests in pushing forward any policy change. As previously discussed, Xi's family

> *Little is really known about what the man expected to lead China for the next decade thinks about ethnic policy*

background might augur a "softer approach" to minority issues or, at least, to the Tibet problem. Early signs, however, seem to suggest that Xi will follow his predecessors in emphasizing ethnic and national unity.

Xi has, since coming to office, spoken repeatedly of the Chinese dream (中国梦). In November 2012 he identified "the great revival of the Chinese nation/race" as the shared dream of the Chinese people (Renmin Ribao 2013: 12). He returned to this subject in March 2013 during his inaugural speech as Chinese president. In his relatively brief remarks Xi spoke of the necessity of "walking the Chinese road," "cultivating the Chinese spirit," and "consolidating Chinese power," making the collective nature of his vision clear through his use of unity (团结) ten times in the short address (Ibid. 3–7).

China Dream is also the title of PLA colonel and NDU researcher Liu Mingfu's (2010) controversial book. This work called for China to openly compete with the United States for global power. While not the first to employ the phrase, Liu's book echoes the same themes as Xi's narrative. Moreover Liu Mingfu cites Sun Yat-sen in his praise of the

Chinese people's assimilative powers (同化力) and the creation of the world's first state-race (国族). These are examples of what William Callahan (2013: 99) calls the "yellow supremacism" running through Liu's writings as well as through the thinking of many others in China.

The broader implications of Xi Jinping's "Chinese dream" for non-Han minorities and ethnic policy are unclear at this stage. Woeser (2013) has claimed there is no room for Tibetans in this Han-centric vision for the future. Meanwhile the new head of the SEAC, Wang Zhengwei (ethnically Hui), has stressed its inclusive message: "In making this dream a reality we must go a step further in our ethnic work and better mobilize and coalesce the fifty-six ethnic groups, unflinchingly walking the Chinese road, cultivating the mighty Chinese spirit, and bringing China's formidable power into play—this is how we pursue, unify, and realize the Chinese dream" (Xinhua 2013).

During his first interview as SEAC chief, Wang spoke of China's ethnic work entering a new era of "significant transformation" without mentioning any specific policy initiatives. He also stressed that "ethnic unity is like air and sunshine; we benefit from it without knowing it, and it would be disastrous to lose" (Ibid.).

There are hints of a desire for policy innovation in the SEAC's annual grant-based research agenda. Topics for 2013 place far more emphasis on fresh thinking in an altered, post-Eighteenth Party Congress, environment. There are twenty-four mentions of new (新) things such as "new demands, new policies, and new strategies" for "new circumstances and new problems" in this six-page document. These mentions include two addressing research into new content and methods (新内容, 新途径) and administrative and structural reform (行政体制改革) of the system of regional ethnic autonomy (SEAC 2012).

There are indications that Xi and his supporters view Singapore, with its 'Asian values,' as a suitable model for managing ethnic relations in China

The nationalistic tone of Xi Jinping's interpretation of the Chinese dream is increasingly evident and suggests that his administration will insist on indigenous models of policy reform and innovation. There are indications that Xi and his supporters view Singapore, with its "Asian values," as a suitable model for managing ethnic relations in China. It was reported in late 2012 that Xi personally endorsed a ten-part China Central Television (CCTV) documentary on the city-state's model of governance. The documentary series will include an episode on ethnic policy tentatively titled "Melting Diverse Ethnic Groups."

The series is the brainchild of General Liu Yazhou. Several sources have speculated that the series might serve as a "blueprint" for the new administration (Huang 2012; Peh 2012). *The New York Times* cites an unnamed source as saying that, following a series of meetings between former Singaporean President Lee Kuan Yew, Xi Jinping, and Jiang Zemin during the summer of 2010, Xi and Jiang agreed to "try to adopt the Singapore model down the road" (Wong and Ansfield 2012).

What can Singapore teach China about ethnic policy? A great deal, according to Professor Zheng Yongnian, director of the influential East Asian Institute (EAI) at the National University of Singapore. Zheng has long been critical of the CPC's ethnic policies, and enjoys good access to top Chinese thinkers and policymakers. He agrees with Ma Rong and Hu Angang in arguing that China's current policies foster ethnic segregation and block the ethnic interactions and solidarity necessary for social stability and national harmony. Following the 7/5 Incident, Zheng warned that, if the CPC does not squarely face this policy crisis, ethnic conflict will increase and the West will seize on the issue to "pin down" China's geostrategic ambitions (Zheng 2009a; 2009b).

Together with Shan Wei (a colleague at EAI), Zheng puts forward Singapore as a positive model for ethnic-policy reform. Unlike China's current approach, Singapore stresses national interest and equality over narrow-group interests and individual rights. The city-state closely monitors ethnic and religious practices while fostering a shared sense of national belonging through a series of explicitly integrationist policies. Zheng concludes that Singapore's experience suggests that China must urgently strengthen its collective national identity, gradually scale back and then eliminate its system of regional ethnic autonomy, and reduce the social and economic gap between the minorities and the Han. It may do so by strengthening mobility, Putonghua education, and interethnic collaboration, among other initiatives (Zheng and Shan 2010).

Many CPC leaders clearly admire what they perceive to be Singapore's recent success in fostering interethnic cohesion and national belonging among its diverse population. There are those within the party who believe this uniquely "East Asian approach," as opposed to Western-style multiculturalism, is better suited to China's cultural and political context. This belief was expressed in a lead article in *Study Times* in the weeks prior to the Eighteenth Party Congress (Song 2012).

Concluding Thoughts

Predicting the future direction of ethnic policy in a political system as opaque as China's is fraught with difficulties. Many a "China prediction" has proven wrong or, at the least, significantly premature.

As discussed, current indicators point to an emerging consensus on the need for ethnic-policy reform. Leading public intellectuals and some CPC officials are now openly calling for new measures to strengthen interethnic cohesiveness and national integration, although opinion still varies on the best methods for achieving this goal. Those calling for change now represent the mainstream, veteran ethnic policy watcher Naran Bilik (forthcoming) recently admitted.

Yet, any radical shift in policy, such as the scrapping of regional ethnic autonomy or ending of minority preferences, is unlikely over the short-to-medium term. Even if the political will exists at the top of the CPC leadership, ethnic policy remains a relatively low priority and the complexities of the Chinese political system make any bold new initiatives problematic.

Moreover, regime stability—the CPC's abiding focus—requires social stability. This means that increased security efforts in frontier regions, such as the expanding "grid management" (网格化管理) system of high-tech surveillance and control (HRW 2013), are more likely than any major rethinking of current ethnic policy and theory.

With the change in leadership, however, small-but-significant adjustments in policy and

Small-but-significant adjustments in policy and rhetoric are possible as the CPC attempts to strengthen social cohesiveness

rhetoric are possible as the CPC attempts to strengthen social cohesiveness and its legitimacy among Han communities in the west as a part of its larger agenda of "stability maintenance." These adjustments could include the removal of ethnic status from third-generation identification cards; the intensification of the study and use of China's official Putonghua language and of patriotic education; and increased ethnic mobility as a part of any changes to the household-registration system.

Simply put, while the current political system remains intact, only subtle shifts in emphasis rather than any major overhaul of ethnic policy may be expected. Reformers (both inside and outside the system) largely agree that change needs to proceed through slow step-by-step consensus building if China hopes to avoid such unintended consequences as increased ethnic violence or, even worse, separatist activities.

Furthermore, any sweeping changes to current policy would require major amendment to the PRC Constitution and would likely damage the CPC's legitimacy and reputation in the eyes of many ethnic minorities as well as the international community. However, should systematic ethnic unrest become widespread, the CPC could be forced into more fundamental changes. This might occur if Han resentment over perceived reverse ethnic discrimination continues to mount in Xinjiang and other regions (see Cliff 2012).

The "second generation of ethnic policies" envisioned by Hu Angang would likely require the collapse of the CPC and China's existing political system to be implemented. It took the demise of the USSR to pave the way for reformists such as Valery Tishkov (a Russian equivalent to Ma Rong) to reshape ethnic policies in the Russian Federation, despite the fact that past policies continue to complicate new initiatives in Russia (Rutland 2010).

If long-term change in China's ethnic policies is inevitable, as Ma Rong and others now believe, the process will be nonlinear and protracted. Yet, any adjustments will most certainly seek to move China in the direction of a more cohesive body politic at the expense of *minzu*-based rights and autonomy. As a result, ethnic conflicts and contradictions will increase before China sees any—if there is to be any—improvement in ethnic relations.

Endnotes

1. The Chinese term *minzu* is exceptionally polysemic and has been used to gloss a wide range of concepts that are largely distinct in English (e.g., ethnic group, nation, nationality, people, or race). *Minzu* is glossed in this study as "ethnicity" or "ethnic group" when it clearly refers to one of China's fifty-six officially recognizing *minzu* groups and as "nation" or "race" when referring to the Chinese nation/race as a collective identity as in *Zhonghua minzu*. Individual *minzu* groups were previously identified in English as "nationalities" but now are increasing identified as "ethnic groups."

2. Roland Soong has aggregated Chinese and foreign reporting on the 7/5 Incident at http://www.zonaeuropa.com/20090706_1.htm

3. Each of the subsequent work reports (2011-13) have included either the phrase "persist with and perfect the system of regional ethnic autonomy" (坚持和完善民族区域自治制度) or "implement the law on regional ethnic autonomy" (贯彻民族区域自治法).

4. Robbie Barnett is thanked for noting this meeting and providing an English summary of its proceedings. All quotes are from the English translation—however they have been checked against the original Chinese text available at http://iea.cass.cn/content-BA0810-2012031609383390681.htm

5. Hao Shiyuan's essays, and other articles both for and against a second generation of ethnic policies, have been collected at www.mzb.com.cn/html/Home/folder/292573-1.htm

6. For example, see http://www.mzb.com.cn/html/Home/node/292573-1.htm; http://cnpolitics.org/2012/09/cn-us-su-ethnical-policy; or http://cnpolitics.org/2012/05/56-ethnic-groups/

7. See http://vote.weibo.com/vid=491693

8. All searches were conducted on May 6, 2013, and may be replicated at http://index.baidu.com

9. Ma Rong is an uncommon name in China and there are no other similarly surnamed individuals in China with such a significant online and public profile.

10. The top-page banner was removed during the spring of 2013, but the special webpage remains at http://www.mzb.com.cn/html/Home/node/292573-1.htm

Bibliography

AFP. 2009. "China Denies Government Policy Reason for Urumqi Riots," *AFP*, July 21. http://www.channelnewsasia.com/stories/afp_asiapacific/view/443778/1/.html.

Ai Weiwei. 2008. "Xizang Shijian Zhengming Zhongguo Shaoshu Minzu Zhengce Shibai" [The Tibet Incident Proves That China's Ethnic Minority Policies Have Failed]. *Deguo Zhi Sheng*, March 18. http://www.observechina.net/info/ArtShow.asp?ID=48628.

Alia. 2012. "An Unbelievably Expensive Piece of Xinjiang Nut Cake and What It Tells About the Ethnic Policy in China." *Offbeat China*, December 4. http://offbeatchina.com/an-unbelievably-expensive-piece-of-xinjiang-nut-cake-and-what-it-tells-about-the-ethnic-policy-in-china.

Barnett, Robert. 2009. "The Tibet Protests of Spring, 2008." *China Perspectives* 3: 6–23.

Barry, Brian. 2001. *Culture and Equality*. Cambridge, UK: Polity.

Bequelin, Nicholas. 2012. "Ethnic Unrest in China: The View from Beijing." Public Lecture at The Weatherhead East Asian Institute, Columbia University, September 12. https://itunes.apple.com/us/itunes-u/weatherhead-east-asian-institute/id534934901.

Berlinf. 2009. "Chinese Ethnic Policies and the Affirmative Action." *Fool's Mountain*, July 7. http://blog.foolsmountain.com/2009/07/07/chinese-ethnic-policies-and-the-affirmative-action-one-rationale-two-failures/.

Bhalla, A.S., and Dan Luo. 2013. *Poverty and Exclusion of Minorities in China and India*. New York: Palgrave Macmillan.

Bilik, Naran. Forthcoming. "How Do You Say 'China' in Mongolian?" In *Minority Education in China*, edited by James Leibold and Chen Yangbin. Hong Kong: Hong Kong University Press.

Bovington, Gardner. 2010. *The Uyghurs*. New York: Columbia University Press.

Callahan, William. 2013. *China Dreams*. New York: Oxford University Press.

Cao Wuxing. 2012. "Qin Hui Zhengzhou 'Zhongyuan Lundao' Tan Minzu Guanxi" [Qin Hui Touches on Ethnic Relations When Discussing the 'China Model' in Zhengzhou]. *Radio France International (Chinese Ed.)*, January 6. http://www.chinese.rfi.fr/中国/20120106-秦晖郑州"中原论道"谈民族关系.

Carlson, Aubrey. 2009. "Minority Policy: Xinjiang Riots Spark Debate Over Reforming the System." *Wikileaks: US State Department Cables*, December 11. http://www.cablegatesearch.net/cable.php?id=09BEIJING3314.

Castells, Manuel. 2010. *The Power of Identity*. 2nd ed. West Sussex, UK: Wiley-Blackwell.

CECC. 2010a. "Central Leaders hold Forum on Xinjiang, Stress Development and Stability as Dual Goals." Congressional Executive Commission on China, July 8. http://www.cecc.gov/pages/virtualAcad/index.phpd?showsingle=141407

———. 2010b. "Communist Party Leadership Outlines 2010–2020 'Tibet Work' Priorities at 'Fifth Forum'." Congressional Executive Commission on China, March 9. http://www.cecc.gov/pages/virtualAcad/index.phpd?showsingle=135152

Chan, Minnie. 2013. "China's New Ethnic Affairs Commissioner 'Has Little Power.'" *South China Morning Post*, March 20. http://www.scmp.com/news/china/article/1194988/chinas-new-ethnic-affairs-commissioner-has-little-power.

Chen Fang. 2012. "Xiangba Pingcuo" (Qiangba Puncog). *Huangfeng Wang*, March 28. http://news.ifeng.com/mainland/detail_2012_03/28/13497187_2.shtml.

Cheng Li. 2008. "Ethnic Minority Elites in China's Party-State Leadership." *China Leadership Monitor* 25: 1–13.

———. 2011. "Introduction." In *China in 2020: A New Type of Superpower*, xv–xl. Washington, DC: Brookings Institution Press.

Cheng Yinghong. 2011. "From Campus Racism to Cyber Racism." *The China Quarterly* 207: 561–79.

Choi Chi-yuk. 2013. "CPPCC Chair Heads Xinjiang, Tibet Affairs Groups." *South China Morning Post*, June 4. http://www.scmp.com/news/china/article/1252832/cppcc-chair-heads-xinjiang-tibet-affairs-groups

Choi Chi-yuk and Mimi Lau. 2012. "Expansion of Central Committee Secretariat May Reflect Ethnic Unrest." *South China Morning Post*, November 19. http://www.scmp.com/news/china/article/1083426/expansion-central-committee-secretariat-may-reflect-ethnic-unrest.

Cliff, Thomas. 2012. "The Partnership of Stability in Xinjiang." *The China Journal* 68: 79–105.

Connor, Walker. 1984. *The National Question in Marxist-Leninist Theory and Strategy*. Princeton, NJ: Princeton University Press.

Cui Zhiyuan. 2009. "Cong Aodili Makesi Zhuyi Xuepai De Feiditu Minzu Faren Lilun Kan Zhongguo Minzu Zhengce" [China's Ethnic Policies in Light of the Austrian Marxists' Non-Territorial Ethnic-Legal Theory]. Powerpoint slides from public lecture, New York University. http://www.strongwindpress.com/ppt/tuijian/CuiNYU.ppt.

Davies, Gloria. 2007. *Worrying About China.* Cambridge, MA: Harvard University Press.

Deng Yuwen. 2012. "What Kind of Democracy Do We Need?" *China Elections and Governance,* September 9. http://chinaelectionsblog.net/?p=20736.

Dikötter, Frank. 1992. *The Discourse of Race in Modern China.* London: Hurst & Co.

Dreyer, June Teufel. 1999. "China, the Monocultural Paradigm." *Orbis* (Fall): 581–97.

Duara, Prasenjit. 1995. *Rescuing History from the Nation.* Chicago: University of Chicago Press.

Fei Xiaotong. 1988. "Plurality and Unity in the Configuration of the Chinese People." The Tanner Lectures on Human Values, The University of Hong Kong. http://tannerlectures.utah.edu/lectures/documents/fei90.pdf.

Feng Chongyi. 2010. "Charter 08, the Troubled History and Future of Chinese Liberalism." *The Asia-Pacific Journal* 2.1. http://www.japanfocus.org/-feng-chongyi/3285.

Ford, Peter. 2012. "Fight Over Snack in China Lights Up Blogosphere." *The Christian Science Monitor,* December 4. http://www.csmonitor.com/World/Asia-Pacific/2012/1204/Fight-over-snack-in-China-lights-up-blogosphere.

Freeman, Carla. 2013. "From 'Blood Transfusion' to 'Harmonious Development.'" *Journal of Current Chinese Affairs* 41.4: 11–44.

Gladney, Dru. 2004. *Dislocating China.* Chicago: Chicago University Press.

Goldman, Merle, and Timothy Cheek. 1987. "Introduction." In *China's Intellectuals and the State,* edited by Merle Goldman, Timothy Cheek, and Carol Lee Harmin, 1–22. Cambridge, MA: Council of East Asian Studies at Harvard University.

Gongmen Law Research Center. 2009. "An Investigative Report Into the Social and Economic Causes of the 3/14 Incident in Tibetan Areas." *International Campaign for Tibet,* June 1. http://www.savetibet.org/media-center/ict-news-reports/bold-report-beijing-scholars-reveals-breakdown-china's-tibet-policy.

Guan Yin. 2007. *Zuqun Zhengzhi* [*Ethnic Politics*]. Beijing: Zhongyang Minzu Daxue Chubanshe.

Guo Qinghai. 2009. "'Lingba Xianzhang' Yu Lianbang Gonghe" ['Charter 08' and Federalism]. *Beijing Zhi Chun,* February 27. http://beijingspring.com/bj2/2009/120/2009227105335.htm.

Hao Shiyuan. 2005. "Gou Jian Shehui Zhuyi Hexie Shehui Yu Minzu Guanxi" [Relations Among Nationalities and the Building of a Harmonious Society of Socialism]. *Minzu Yanjiu* 3: 1–14.

———. 2012. "Sulian Shibao, Meiguo Ye Wei Chenggong" [The USSR Failed, But America Has Also Yet to Succeed]. *21ccom.net,* May 30. http://www.21ccom.net/articles/qqsw/qqgc/article_2012053060752.html.

Harrell, Stevan. 1995. "Civilizing Projects and the Reaction to Them." In *Cultural Encounters on China's Ethnic Frontiers,* edited by Melissa Brown, 3–36. Seattle, WA: University of Washington.

He Liangliang. 2012. "Zhongguo Shaoshu Minzu Ronghe Bu Tong Yu Hanhua" [The Fusion of China's Ethnic Minorities is Not the Same as Assimilation]. *Fenghuang Weishi*, February 17. http://news.ifeng.com/opinion/phjd/sh/detail_2012_02/18/12603835_0.shtml.

Hong Sha. 2012. "Jiazu Fojiao Yuanyuan Shen" [Buddhism Runs Deep Within the Clan]. *Duowei Xinwen*, November 15. http://china.dwnews.com/news/2012-11-15/58962449.html.

Hu Ping. 2009. "Tantan Minzu Zizhi Wenti" [Talking About the Problem of Ethnic Autonomy]. *Beijing Zhi Chun*, May. http://blog.boxun.com/hero/200907/xianzhang/6_1.shtml.

———. 2012. "Zhonggong Yao Tiaozheng Minzu Zhengce Ma?" [Does China Need to Readjust its Ethnic Policy?]. *Radio Free Asia*, February 20. http://www.rfa.org/mandarin/pinglun/hp-02202012131802.html.

Hu Angang and Hu Lianhe. 2011. "Dierdai Minzu Zhengce" [Second Generation of Ethnic Policies]. *Xinjiang Shifan Daxue Xuebao (Zhexue Shehui Kexue Bao)* 32.5: 1–13.

Huang, Cary. 2012. "Communist Party Journal Suggests it Could Learn from Singapore's PAP." *South China Morning Post*, October 23. http://www.scmp.com/news/china/article/1067561/communist-party-journal-suggests-it-could-learn-singapores-pap.

Huang Yuanshan and Zhang Wenshan. 2007. "Minzu Quyu Zizhiquan De Xianzheng Jieshi" [Explaining the Right of Regional Ethnic Autonomy in the Constitution]. *Guangxi Minzu Yanjiu* 1: 12–18.

HRW. 2013. " China: Alarming New Surveillance, Security in Tibet." *Human Rights Watch*, March 20. http://www.hrw.org/news/2013/03/20/china-alarming-new-surveillance-security-tibet

ICT. 2013. "New Challenges to Tibet Policy from inside China." *International Campaign for Tibet*, June 27. http://www.savetibet.org/new-challenges-to-tibet-policy-from-inside-china/

Jacques, Martin. 2009. *When China Rules the World*. New York: The Penguin Press.

Jia Wenshan, Y.T. Lee, and Zhang Haiyang. 2012. "Ethno-Political Conflicts in China." In *Handbook of Ethnic Conflict*, edited by Dan Landis and Rosita Albert, 177–96. New York: Springer.

Johnson, Ian. 2012a. "China Faces New Scandal Over Crash of a Ferrari." *The New York Times*, September 3. http://www.nytimes.com/2012/09/04/world/asia/after-ling-jihuas-demotion-news-of-sons-crash-in-ferrari.html.

———. 2012b. "Learning How to Argue." *NYR Blog*, March 1. http://www.nybooks.com/blogs/nyrblog/2012/mar/02/learning-how-argue-interview-ran-yunfei/.

Kong Qingdong. 2011a. "Mao Zhuxi Jiu Shi Zui Da De Huofu" [Chairman Mao is the Biggest Living Buddha]. *Hongge Hui Wang*, July 19. http://www.szhgh.com/html/48/n-3148.html.

———. 2011b. "Zhongguo Jueqi Bixu Xuyao Jiejue De Wu Ge Wenti" [Five Problems That Must be Solved for China's Rise]. Preface to Xu Liang, *Diguo Xingshuai*

Yu Diguo Bianjiang De Bengta [Rise and Fall of Empires and the Collapse of Empires' Border Regions]. Beijing: Falu Chubanshe. http://www.qstheory.cn/jj/jjggyfz/201109/t20110907_108581.htm.

Kong Xie. 2012. "Zhongguo Minzu Zhengce Mianlin Gaibian Yu Tiaozhan" [China's Ethnic Policies are Facing Change and Challenges]. *Duowei Boke*, February 19. http://opinion.dwnews.com/news/2012-02-19/58604752.html.

Lam, Willy. 2009. "Jiang Zemin Casts Long Shadow Over National Day Parade." *China Brief*, October 7. http://www.jamestown.org/single/?tx_ttnews[tt_news]=35587.

Leading Group of the SEAC. 2012. "Ethnic Initiative Since the Sixteenth National Congress of the CPC." *Quishi* 4.3. http://english.qstheory.cn/politics/201210/t20121009_185283.htm.

Leibold, James. 2007. *Reconfiguring Chinese Nationalism*. New York: Palgrave Macmillan.

———. 2010a. "More than a Category." *The China Quarterly* 203 (September): 539–59.

———. 2010b. "Sheep in Wolves' Clothing? The Book the Han Nationalists Love to Loath." *The China Beat*, January 7. http://www.thechinabeat.org/?p=1301

———. 2012. "When Will China Have its First Minority President?" *The Atlantic*, November 8. http://www.theatlantic.com/international/archive/2012/11/when-will-china-have-its-first-minority-president/264961/.

Li Datong. 2009a. "China's Tibet: Question with No Answer." *Open Democracy*, April 23. http://www.opendemocracy.net/article/chinas-tibet-question-with-no-answer.

———. 2009b. "Xizang Wenti Yu Jiema?" [Is There a Solution to the Tibet Problem?]. *BBC Chinese Service*, April 7. http://news.bbc.co.uk/chinese/simp/hi/newsid_7980000/newsid_7985400/7985440.stm.

———. 2011. "Yingmei: Neimeng Kangyi Shi Minjian Duonian Yiyuan Suozhi [English Media: Inner Mongolian Protests are Caused by Years of Accumulated Rancor Among the People]. *Duowei Xinwen*, May 31. http://china.dwnews.com/news/2011-05-31/57764336.html.

Li Hong. 2009. "Urumqi Killing is Barbaric." *People's Daily Online*, July 10. http://english.people.com.cn/90002/96743/6697878.html.

Li Xiaoxia. 2004. "Zhongguo Ge Minzu Jian Zuji Hunyin De Xianzhuang Fenxi" [Analysis of the Current State of Interethnic Marriage Among Different Chinese Ethnic Groups]. *Renkou Yanjiu* 3. http://www.xjass.com/shx/content/2008-07/30/content_25784.htm.

Li Yin and Wang Tian. 2012. "Shibada Wei Minzu Gongzuo Zhiming Le Fangxiang" [The Eighteenth Party Congress' Orientation on Ethnic Work]. *Zhongguo Minzu Bao*, November 13. http://www.mzb.com.cn/html/Home/report/344211-1.htm.

Lim, Benjamin, and Frank Daniel. 2012. "Does China's Next Leader Have a Soft Spot for Tibet?" *Reuters*, August 30. http://www.reuters.com/article/2012/08/30/us-china-tibet-xi-idUSBRE87T1G320120830.

Link, Perry, trans. 2009. "China's Charter 08." *New York Review of Books*, January 15. http://www.nybooks.com/articles/archives/2009/jan/15/chinas-charter-08/.

Liu Junning. 2000. "Classical Liberalism Catches on in China." *Journal of Democracy* 11.3: 48–57.

———. 2002. "Liansheng Zizhi" [Provincial Self-Rule]. *Zhanlüe Yu Guanli* 54. http://blog.boxun.com/hero/liujn/31_5.shtml.

———. 2009. "Quxiao Minzu Duoyuan Gongzhi" [Abolishing Minzu: Multivariate Collective Rule]. *BBC Chinese Service*, July 20. http://news.bbc.co.uk/chinese/simp/hi/newsid_8150000/newsid_8158800/8158867.stm.

———. 2011. "The Ancient Roots of Chinese Liberalism." *The Wall Street Journal*, July 6. http://online.wsj.com/article/SB10001424052702304760604576427931129537282.html.

Liu Ling. 2012. "Jianchi Jiben Zhengzhi Zhidu Zai Fazhan Jiejue Minzu Wenti" [Persist in the Basic Political System, Resolve Ethnic Issues Through Development]. The Institute of Ethnology and Anthropology, CASS, February 23. http://iea.cass.cn/content-BA0810-2012031609383390681.htm.

Liu, Melinda. 2012. "Will Beijing's New Leaders Solve the Tibet Crisis?" *Newsweek*, August 15. http://www.thedailybeast.com/newsweek/2012/10/14/will-beijing-s-new-leaders-solve-the-tibet-crisis.html.

Liu Mingfu. 2010. *Zhongguo Meng* [*China Dream*]. Beijing: Zhongguo Youyi Chuban Gongsi.

Liu Xiaobo. 2012. *No Enemies, No Hatred*. Cambridge, MA: The Belknap Press of Harvard University Press.

Liu Yazhou. 2001 [2007]. "The Grand National Strategy." *Chinese Law and Government* 40.2: 13–36.

Ma Rong. 1999. "Zhongguo Ge Minzu Zhijian De Zuji Tonghun" [Interethnic Marriages Among Each of China's Ethnicities]. *Minzu Shehuixue Tongxun*, 16: np.

———. 2007. "A New Perspective in Guiding Ethnic Relations in the Twenty-First Century." *Asian Ethnicity* 8.3: 199–217.

———. 2009a. "The Key to Understanding and Interpreting Ethnic Relations in Contemporary China." *International Institute of Social Studies (ISS)*, November 13.

———. 2009b. "Meiguo Ruhe Chulu 'Minzu Wenti'?" [How Does America Handle the 'Ethnic Question'?]. *Nanfang Zhouwei*, July 16. http://www.infzm.com/content/31554.

———. 2010. "Policies in Ethnic Relations in Contemporary China." Unpublished paper.

———. 2011. "Income Gaps in Economic Development: Differences Among Regions, Occupational Groups and Ethnic Groups." *ProtoSociology* 28: 101–29.

———. 2012. *Zuqun, Minzu Yu Guojia Goujian* [*Ethnicity, Nationality and Nation-Building*]. Beijing: Shehui Kexue Wenxian Chubanshe.

————. 2013. "Guanyu Dangqian Woguo Minzu Wenti de Jinyibu Taolun: Yetan 'Dierdai Minzu Zhengce'." (Further Discussion of our Country's Ethnic Issues: Talk of a 'Second Generation of Ethnic Policies'). *Minzu Shehuixue Yanjiu Tongxun* 127 (January 15): 1-17.

Mackerras, Colin. 2003. *China's Ethnic Minorities and Globalization.* London: RoutledgeCurzon.

————. 2006. "Ethnic Minorities." In *Critical Issues in Contemporary China*, edited by Czeslaw Tubilewicz, 167–91. London: Routledge.

————. 2012. "Causes and Ramifications of the Xinjiang July 2009 Disturbances." *Sociology Study* 2.7: 496-510.

Martin, Terry. 2001. *The Affirmative Action Empire.* Ithaca, NY: Cornell University Press.

Mei Xinyu. 2012. "Weihe Minzu Guangxi Chuxian Bu Hexie? [Why Do Ethnic Relations Appear Un-Harmonious?]. *Wuyou Zhi Xiang,* May 24. http://www.wyzxsd.com/article.php?id=534.

Meng Ke. 2012. "Zangren Zifen, Qiegao Shijian Yu Minzu Zhengce Jiantao" [Tibetan Self-Immolation, the Nut-Cake Incident and Ethnic Policy Thoroughly Discussed], *BBC Chinese Service,* December 21. http://www.bbc.co.uk/zhongwen/simp/chinese_news/2012/12/121221_new_nationality_policy.shtml.

Millward, James. 2009. "Does the 2009 Urumchi Violence Mark a Turning Point?" *Central Asian Survey* 28.4: 347–60.

Mullaney, Thomas. 2011. *Coming to Terms with the Nation.* Berkeley, CA: University of California Press.

Naughton, Barry, and Dali Yang. 2004. *Holding China Together.* Cambridge, UK: Cambridge University Press.

Oriental Daily. 2009. "Shaoguan Wei-Han Da Chongtu" [The Shaoguan Han-Uyghur Riot]. *Dongfang Ribao,* June 29. http://orientaldaily.on.cc/cnt/china_world/20090629/00182_001.html.

Osnos, Evan. 2008. "Angry Youth." *The New Yorker,* July 28. http://www.newyorker.com/reporting/2008/07/28/080728fa_fact_osnos.

Peh Shing Huei. 2012. "CCTV Goes Big on S'pore with 10-Parter." *The Straits Times,* October 26. http://www.straitstimes.com/the-big-story/asia-report/china/story/cctv-goes-big-spore-10-parter-20121026.

Phoenix Weekly. 2012. "Dalu Minzi Shibie Wenti Jiantao" [The Mainland's Ethnic Classification Question Thoroughly Discussed]. *Fenghuang Zhoukan* 9. http://www.ifengweekly.com/display.php?newsId=5237.

Qin Hui. 2012. "'Zuoyou Duoyuanhua' Zui Neng Danhua Minzu Rentong Duoyuanhua" ['Left-Right Pluralism' Can Best Weaken the Plurality of Ethnic Identifications]. *Nanfang Dushi Bao,* March 4. http://www.mzb.com.cn/html/report/278908-2.htm.

Qiu Zhenghai. 2009. "Xinjiang Saoluan Jiqi Chuli De Jidian Guancha" [Several Observations About the Xinjiang Riots and Their Handling]. *Caogen,* July 14. http://www.caogen.com/blog/infor_detail.aspx?ID=90&articleId=15569.

Ran Yunfei. 2008. "Wo Dui Xizang Wenti De Taidu" [My Views on the Tibet Problem]. *BBS.51*, March 20. http://bbs.51.ca/thread-160559-1-1.html.

———. 2009. "Wo Dui Xinjiang Wenti De Kanfa" [My Views on the Xinjiang Problem]. *Xin Shijie Xinwen Wang*, July 9. http://www.newcenturynews .com/Article/gd/200907/20090709233919.html.

Renmin Ribao. 2013. *Zhongguo Meng [The Chinese Dream]*. Beijing: Renmin Chubanshe.

RFA. 2013. "Tibetans Allowed to Openly Revere the Dalai Lama in Two Chinese Provinces." *Radio Free Asia*, June 26. http://www.rfa.org/english/news/tibet/ allowed-06262013180033.html

RFI. 2009. "Zhongguo Zhengfu Jiancheng Minzu Zhengce Zhengque Xuezhe Paichi Wei Tuonian Zhengce" [Chinese Government Insists that the Ethnic Policies that Academics Denounce as an Ostrich Policy are Correct]. *Radio France International (Chinese Ed.)*, July 21. http://www.rfi.fr/actucn/articles/115/ article_14974.asp.

Rutland, Peter. 2010. "Ethnicity Policy in Russia." In *Institutions, Ideas and Leadership in Post-Soviet Russia*, edited by Julia Newton and William Tompson, 116–36. New York: Palgrave Macmillan.

Sautman, Barry. 2010. "Scaling Back Minority Rights?" *Stanford Journal of International Law* 51: 51–120.

———. 2012. "Paved with Good Intentions." *Modern China* 38.1: 10–39.

Schiavenza, Matt. 2013. "China to Tibetans: Stay Put." *The Atlantic*, January 31. http://www.theatlantic.com/international/archive/2013/01/china-to-tibetans-stay-put/272709/.

SCMP. 2013. "Mongol Ally of Incoming Premier to Become Chief of State Council." *The South China Morning Post*, March 18. http://www.scmp.com/news/ china/article/1185815/mongol-ally-incoming-premier-become-chief-state-council.

SEAC. 2012. "Guojia Minwei Bangongting Guanyu Shenbao Guojia Minwei Minzu Wenti Yanjiu Xiangmu 2013 Niandu Keti de Tongzhi" [SEAC General Office Announces Annual 2013 Research Project Topics on Ethnic Issues]. SEAC Website, December 21. http://www.seac.gov.cn/art/2012/12/21/ art_144_174225.html.

Shambaugh, David. 2008. *China's Communist Party*. Berkeley, CA: University of California Press.

Shirk, Susan, ed. 2011. *Changing Media, Changing China*. Oxford, UK: Oxford University Press.

Sima Pingbang. 2009a. "Bai Nian Nei Wancheng 'Zhonghua Minzu' Qudai 56 Zu De Yitong" [Replacing the Unity of 56 Ethnic Groups with a Single 'Chinese Nation' Within 100 Years]. *Fenghuang Blog*, July 9. http://blog.ifeng.com/ article/2911763.html.

———. 2009b. "Gaokao Zhuangyuan Zaojia De Zui Yuan Shi Minzu Youhui Zhengce" [Preferential Minority Policies are the Original Sin Behind the Gaokao

Top-Scorer's Fabrication]. *Sina Blogspot*, July 7. http://blog.sina.com.cn/s/blog_537fd7410100e19e.html~type=v5_one&label=rela_prevarticle.

Song Xiongwei. 2012. "Xinjiapo Jianshe Fuwu Xing Zhengfu De Jingyan" [Singapore's Experience Building a Service-Style Government]. *Xuexi Shibo*, October 22. www.21ccom.net/articles/qqsw/qqgc/article_2012102269467.html.

State Council. 2009. *White Paper: Ethnic Policy and Common Prosperity and Development of All Ethnic Groups*, September 27. http://www.china.org.cn/government/whitepaper/node_7078073.htm.

Tang Wenfang. 2005. *Public Opinion and Political Change in China*. Stanford, CA: Stanford University Press.

TIN. 2012. "Business as Usual." *Tibet Information Network* 188. http://www.tibetinfonet.net/content/update/188.

Wang Hui. 2008. "Modern China Emerged Before its Encounter with the West." *New Perspectives Quarterly* 25.4: 10–15.

———. 2011. "The 'Tibetan Question' East and West." In *The Politics of Imagining Asia*, 136–227. Cambridge, MA: Harvard University Press.

Wang Huning. 2004. *Zhengzhi De Luoji* [*Logic of Politics*]. Shanghai: Shanghai Renmin Chubanshe.

Wang Lixiong. 2008a. "March Incident in Tibet is the Watershed: Roadmap of Tibetan Independence (Chapter One)." *Wang Lixiong Wenku*. http://wlx.sowiki.net//?action=index&cid=2.

———. 2008b. "A True 'Middle-Way' Solution to Tibetan Unrest." *WSI China Security* 4.2: 27–37.

———. 2012. "Chule Zifen, Hai Neng Zuo Shenme?" [Besides Self-Immolation, What Can Be Done?]. *Invisible Tibet*, January 14. http://woeser.middle-way.net/2012/01/blog-post_14.html.

Wang Shaoguang. 2002. "Zhongguo Caizheng Zhuanyi Zhifu De Zhengzhi Luoji" [The Political Logic of Fiscal Transfers in China]. *Zhanlüe Yu Guanli* 3: 47–54.

Wang Xiaodong. 2007. "Wang Xiaodong Diyici Zuoke Hanwang Yu Wangyou Duihua" [Wang Xiaodong's First Dialogue with Netizens and Guest Appearance on Hanwang]. *Hanwang*, August 11. [no longer available]

———. 2009. "Wang Xiaodong Dierci Zuoke Hanwang Yu Wangyou Duihua" [Wang Xiaodong's Second Dialogue with Netizens and Guest Appearance on Hanwang]. *Hanwang*, April 11. [no longer available]

Wang Xin. 2012. "Dangnei 'Neige' Da Bianlian" [Big Changes to the Party's Inner Cabinet]. *Duowei Xinwen*, November 17. http://18.dwnews.com/news/2012-11-17/58965829.html.

Wang Yiyou. 2008. "Qin Hui, Wen Tiejun, Wang Hui Sanren Duihua [A Dialogue Between Qin Hui, Wen Tiejun and Wang Hui]." *Douban*, January 26. http://www.douban.com/group/topic/2548767/.

Wang Xizhe and Liu Xiaobo. 1996. "Zhi Guogong Liangdang De Shuangshi Xuanyan" [20 Point Manifesto for the CPC and KMT]. *Beijing Zhi Chun* 11. http://beijingspring.com/bj2/1996/170/2003127175607.htm.

Wenrui Tiankong. 2008. "Woguo Minzu Zhengce Zhidu Gai Yijing Keburonghuan" [The Reform of Our Country's Ethnic Policies Cannot Be Delayed a Second Further]. *Sina Blogs*, August 2. http://blog.sina.com.cn/lj0621.

Woeser, Tsering. 2012. "'Huchenghe' Yu 'Zhongzu Geli'" ['Moats' and 'Apartheid']. *Woeser Middle Way*, July 25. http://woeser.middle-way.net/2012/07/blog-post_25.html.

———. 2013. "No Room for Tibetans in the Chinese Dream." *Radio Free Asia*, March 5. http://www.rfa.org/english/commentaries/room-03052013153949.html.

Wong, Edward, and Jonathan Ansfield. 2012. "Many Urge Next Leader of China to Liberalize." *The New York Times*, October 21. http://www.nytimes.com/2012/10/22/world/asia/many-urge-chinas-next-leader-to-enact-reform.html.

Wu Yan. 2012. "Minzu Lilun Yanjiu Redian Wenti Xueshu Yantaohui Zaijing Juxing" [Academic Symposium on the Hot Topic of Minzu Theory Opens in Beijing]. *Zhongguo Minzu Bao*, April 13. http://www.mzb.com.cn/html/node/294149-1.htm.

Xiao Sanza. 2012. *Zuoyouweinan* [*Predicament*]. Fujian: Fujian Jiaoyu Chubanseh. Extracted at http://news.boxun.com/forum/201301/lilun/3081.shtml.

Xinhua. 2010. "Zhengfu Gongzuo Baogao" [Government Work Report], March 15. http://news.xinhuanet.com/politics/2010-03/15/content_13174348.htm

———. 2011a. "Full Text of Speech by Xi Jinping at Tibet's Peaceful Liberation Anniversary Conference," China.org, July 19. http://www.china.org.cn/china/2011-07/19/content_23023375.htm.

———. 2011b. "Life Expectancy in Tibet Nearly Doubled Over Last Six Decades." *People's Daily Online*, July 12. http://english.peopledaily.com.cn/90001/90776/90785/7436448.html.

———. 2013. Wang Zhengwei Minzu Gongzuo Redian Nandian Shou Xinhuashe Zhuanfang [Special Interview with Wang Zhengwei on the Hotspots and Difficult Points in Ethnic Work]. SEAC, April 19. http://www.seac.gov.cn/art/2013/4/19/art_31_182155.html.

Xu Yan. 2010. "Women Dou Shuyu 'Zhonghua Minzu'" [We All Belong to the 'Chinese Nation']. *Huanqiu Renwu*, December 15. http://opinion.people.com.cn/GB/51863/13488774.html.

Yan Xuetong. 2009. "Jiaqiang Minzu Guojia Jiangou Shi Zhongguo Weilai De Zhongda Shiming" [Strengthening the Fabric of the Nation-State is a Weighty Mission for China's Future]. *Zhongguo Shehui Kexue Bao*, July 3. http://theory.people.com.cn/GB/49150/49152/9591710.html. http://www.caogen.com/blog/infor_detail.aspx?ID=163&articleId=16139.

Ye Bing. 2009. "Wang Yang Tan Zhongguo Minzu Zhengce Wenti" [Wang Yang Talks About the Problem of China's Ethnic Policies]. *VOA Chinese*, July 31. http://www.voanews.com/chinese/news/a-21-2009-07-31-voa41-60881482.html.

Yi Fuxian. 2009. "Cong Xiangxi Minzu Renkou Goucheng Kan Zhongguo Minzu Zhengce De Zouxiang" [Looking at the Direction of China's Ethnic Policies From the Perspective of the Ethnic Population of Western Hunan]. *Caogen*, August 17.

Yu Shiyu. 2009. "Xinjiang Dongluan He Yilang Dongluan De Duibi [Comparing the Xinjiang Turmoil with the Iran Turmoil]. *Caogen*, July 13. http://www.caogen.com/blog/infor_detail.aspx?ID=93&articleId=15548.

Zhao Tingyang. 2005. *Tianxia Tixi [The Tianxia System]*. Nanjing: Jiangsu Jiaoyu Chubanshe.

Zheng Yongnian. 2009a. "Xinjiang, Xizang Wenti Yu Zhongguo De Guoji Guanxi" [The Xinjiang and Tibet Problem and China's International Relations]. *Nanfang Ribao*, July 28. http://opinion.nfdaily.cn/content/2009-07/28/content_5433512.htm.

———. 2009b. "Zhongguo Shaoshu Minzu Zhengce De Wenti Daodi Zai Nail?" [Where is the Problem with China's Ethnic Minority Policy?]. *Lianhe Zaobao*, July 21. http://www.zaobao.com/special/china/cnpol/pages2/cnpol090721c.shtml.

Zheng Yongnian and Shan Wei. 2010. "Jiang-Zang Saoluan Yuanyin Pouxi Ji Xinjiapo Jingyan De Qishi" [An Analysis of the Tibet and Xinjiang Riots in Light of the Experience of Singapore]. *Dongya Lunwen* 77. www.eai.nus.edu.sg/CWP77.pdf.

Zhu Weiqun. 2012. "Dui Dangqian Minzu Lingyu Wenti De Jidian Sikao" [Some Thoughts on Issues Related to Current Ethnic Problems]. *Xuexi Shibao*, February 13. http://www.studytimes.com.cn/2012/02/13/01/01_51.htm.

Zhu Yuchao and Dongyan Blachford. 2012. "Economic Expansion, Marketization, and Their Social Impact on China's Ethnic Minorities in Xinjiang and Tibet." *Asia Survey* 52.4: 714–33.

Acknowledgments

The author would like to thank the East-West Center, the editors and editorial staff of its *Policy Studies* publication series, and the anonymous reviewers for their encouragement and valuable criticisms and suggestions on earlier drafts.

Over the course of the project the following individuals have provided helpful assistance, suggestions, and comments: Dru Gladney, Barry Sautman, Saul Thomas, Chen Yangbin, He Baogang, William Callahan, Colin Mackerras, Timothy Grose, Ma Rong, Cheng Yinghong, Agnieszka Joniak-Lüthi, Tom Cliff, Antonio Terrone, Enze Han, Robbie Barnett, David Brophy, Kerry Brown, Ben Hillman, Naran Bilik, Peh Shing Huei, Kate Axup, and my anonymous informants.

I would like to also thank the participants of the 2013 Australian National University/Columbia University workshop held in San Diego on "Ethnic Conflict in Western China" and also those of the 2013 IES seminar held in Beijing, both venues where some of these ideas were earlier presented and discussed.

Some of the material draws on short essays published in *China Brief, China Policy Brief, The Diplomat, Tea Leaf Nation,* and *The Atlantic.* Here I would like to acknowledge the assistance and feedback provided by Philippa Jones, David Kelly, Harry Kazianis, Peter Mattis, and David Wertime.

All opinions and any mistakes or shortcomings remain the author's alone.

www.ingramcontent.com/pod-product-compliance
Lightning Source LLC
Chambersburg PA
CBHW050559280326
41933CB00011B/1905